PUT IT IN WRITING!
NASW PRESS CALL FOR BOOK PROPOSALS

NASW Press publishes high-quality professional books of relevance to social workers and other professionals in social welfare and the human services.

We welcome proposals on a variety of topics and seek submissions for scholarly works, textbooks, reference works, practice books, and guidebooks.

In general, **NASW Press** focuses on publishing books that contribute to the advancement of knowledge and practice in social work.

PROPOSAL REQUIREMENTS

Prospective authors should submit a completed NASW Press Book Proposal Packet, which they may obtain by contacting Acquisitions Editor Stella Donovan or downloading it from the "Tools for Authors" section of the NASW Press Web site (http://naswpress.org/authors/guidelines/03-books.html). This brief packet contains two sections: one with questions about the book's author(s), content, and target market, and one that explains the required attachments (curriculum vitae, table of contents, and sample chapter).

One electronic copy (written in Microsoft Word) should be sent to Stella Donovan, acquisitions editor (sdonovan@naswdc.org). **Please type "Book Proposal Packet" in the subject line.** For more detailed information, visit the **Author Center** at **www.naswpress.org**.

NASW PRESS

BKPR14

EDITOR-IN-CHIEF
Stephen H. Gorin, PhD, *Plymouth State University, Plymouth, NH*

PRESIDENT
Darrell P. Wheeler, PhD, MPH, ACSW

CHIEF EXECUTIVE OFFICER
Angelo McClain, PhD, LICSW

EDITORIAL BOARD
Samuel S. Flint, *Indiana University Northwest, Gary*
Sarah Gehlert, *Washington University, St. Louis*
Valire Carr Copeland, *University of Pittsburgh*
Nancy Giunta, *Hunter College, City University of New York*
Christine M. Rine, *Buffalo State, State University of New York*

EDITOR, PRACTICE FORUM
Sherry Cummings, *University of Tennessee, Nashville*

EDITOR, BOOK REVIEWS
Christine M. Rine, *Buffalo State, State University of New York*

HEALTH & SOCIAL WORK EDITORS
2002–2006 Colleen M. Galambos
1998–2002 Sharon M. Keigher
1995–1998 Dennis L. Poole
1990–1994 Judith W. Ross
1986–1990 Thomas Owen Carlton*
1983–1986 Barbara Berkman
1979–1983 Rosalie Kane
1975–1979 Beatrice Phillips
*Deceased

CONSULTING EDITORS
David L. Albright, *University of Missouri, Columbia;* Heidi Allen, *Columbia University, New York;* Pablo Arriaza, *University of New Hampshire, Manchester;* Kelly Aschbrenner, *Dartmouth Medical School, Concord, NH;* Wendy Auslander, *Washington University, St. Louis;* Sara S. Bachman, *Boston University;* Nancy L. Beckerman, *Yeshiva University, New York;* Melissa Bellin, *University of Maryland, Baltimore;* Gauri Bhattacharya, *Jackson State University, Jackson, MS;* Thomas J. Blakely, *Touchstone Innovarè, Grand Rapids, MI;* Robin P. Bonifas, *Arizona State University, Phoenix;* Teri Browne, *University of South Carolina, Columbia;* Page W. Buck, *West Chester University, West Chester, PA;* Karen Bullock, *North Carolina State University, Raleigh;* Colleen L. Campbell, *Department of Veterans Affairs, Gainesville, FL;* Rebecca Cantor, *Harvard University, Cambridge, MA;* Iraida Carrion, *University of South Florida, Tampa;* Wallace Chi Ho Chan, *Chinese University of Hong Kong;* Tyrone C. Cheng, *University of Alabama, Tuscaloosa;* Brittney R. Chesworth, *Vitas Innovative Hospice Care, Sacramento, CA;* Kameri Christy, *University of Arkansas, Fayetteville;* Laurene Clossey, *East Stroudsburg University, PA;* Portia L. Cole, *Joint Commission on Health Care, Richmond, VA;* Jacqueline Corcoran, *Virginia Commonwealth University, Richmond;* Llewellyn J. Cornelius, *University of Georgia, Athens;* Teresa V. Crowe, *Gallaudet University, Washington, DC;* Sherry Cummings, *University of Tennessee, Nashville;* Judith W. Dekle, *Department of Defense, Alexandria, VA;* Amanda Evans, *Florida Gulf Coast University, Ft. Myers;* Patricia A. Findley, *Rutgers, State University of New Jersey, New Brunswick;* L. Ashley Gage, *University of Nebraska at Kearney;* Eric Garland, *University of Utah, Salt Lake City;* Gina B. Gaston, *University of Illinois at Chicago;* Elissa D. Giffords, *Long Island University, Brookville, NY;* Kevin M. Gorey, *University of Windsor, Ontario, Canada;* Sarah Graden, *University of Pennsylvania, Philadelphia;* Johnnie Hamilton-Mason, *Simmons College, Boston;* Elizabeth F. Hoffler, *Prevent Cancer Foundation, Alexandria, VA;* Pilar S. Horner, *Michigan State University, East Lansing;* Denise A. Humm-Delgado, *Simmons College, Boston;* Emily S. Ihara, *George Mason University, Fairfax, VA;* Ramona R. Ivy, *North Carolina State University, Raleigh;* Reid Jacobs, *Agape Healthcare, Denver;* Kim Jaffee, *Wayne State University, Detroit;* Minchao Jin, *Washington University, St. Louis;* Dawn M. Joosten, *University of Southern California, Los Angeles;* Sandra Kopels, *University of Illinois at Urbana–Champaign;* Wynne S. Korr, *University of Illinois at Urbana–Champaign;* Brian Trung Lam, *California State University, Long Beach;* Kristina S. Lind, *Plymouth State University, Plymouth, NH;* Sana Loue, *Case Western Reserve University, Cleveland;* R. William Lusenhop, *University of New Hampshire, Durham;* Stephen Magura, *Western Michigan University, Kalamazoo;* Kamilah Majied, *Howard University, Washington, DC;* Flavio F. Marsiglia, *Arizona State University, Phoenix;* Tina Maschi, *Fordham University, New York;* Sarah E. McMahon, *Rutgers, State University of New Jersey, New Brunswick;* Anna R. McPhatter, *Morgan State University, Baltimore;* Eva Margarita Moya, *University of Texas at El Paso;* Shari Munch, *Rutgers, State University of New Jersey, New Brunswick;* Megan Moore, *University of Washington, Seattle;* Marlys R. Peck, *University of Central Missouri, Warrensburg;* Tam Perry, *Wayne State University, Detroit, MI;* James E. Phelan, *Department of Veterans Affairs, Columbus, OH;* Amanda R. Reedy, *Eastern Washington University, Cheney;* Elaine S. Rinfrette, *Edinboro University of Pennsylvania;* Anissa Rogers, *University of Portland, Oregon;* Diana Rowan, *University of North Carolina, Charlotte;* Betty J. Ruth, *Boston University;* Andrew W. Safyer, *Adelphi University, Garden City, NY;* Patricia W. Saleeby, *Southern Illinois University, Carbondale;* Daniel Sebbag, *Yeshiva University, New York;* Samuel E. Simon, *Mathematica Policy Research, Inc., Cambridge, MA;* Amanda G. Sisselman, *Lehman College, Bronx, NY;* William Patrick Sullivan, *Indiana University, Indianapolis;* Betty Surbeck, *West Chester University, West Chester, PA;* Maria E. Torres, *Brandeis University, Waltham, MA;* Sabrina W. Tyuse, *St. Louis University;* Vikki L. Vandiver, *University of Alabama, Tuscaloosa;* Angela Wangari Walter, *Boston University;* Karla T. Washington, *University of Missouri, Columbia;* Sherrie L. Wilcox, *University of Southern California, Los Angeles;* Catherine Worthington, *University of Victoria, Victoria, British Columbia, Canada;* Paula Yuma, *University of Texas at Austin;* Michaela L. Zajicek-Farber, *Catholic University of America, Washington, DC;* Jennifer R. Zelnick, *Touro College, New York;* Joan Levy Zlotnik, *Social Work Policy Institute, NASW, Washington, DC;* Sarah Rebecca Zlotnik, *PolicyLab, Children's Hospital of Philadelphia;* Daniyal Zuberi, *University of Toronto*

NASW PRESS STAFF
Cheryl Y. Bradley, *Publisher;* Julie Gutin, *Managing Editor;* Sarah Lowman, *Senior Editor;* Sharon Fletcher, *Marketing Manager;* Kiera White, *Marketing Coordinator;* Bill Cathey, *Production and Media Specialist;* Tracey Hawkins, *Circulation Coordinator;* Helen C. Williams, *Circulation Coordinator;* Lisa Brown, *Administrative Assistant*

Health & Social Work (ISSN 0360-7283) is a professional journal committed to improving social work practice and extending knowledge in the field of health. Health is defined broadly to include both physical and mental health. The editorial board welcomes manuscripts that deal with all aspects of health that are of professional concern to social workers—for example, practice, social policy and planning, legislative issues, innovation, and research. Statements of fact and opinion in the articles in *Health & Social Work* are those of the authors and contributors, not of NASW Press or Oxford University Press, and do not necessarily reflect the official position of NASW or Oxford University Press. Neither NASW Press nor Oxford University Press makes any representation, express or implied, regarding the accuracy of the material in this journal and cannot accept any legal responsibility or liability for any errors or omissions that may be made. The reader should make his or her own evaluation as to the appropriateness or otherwise of any experimental technique described.

In the interest of accurate and unbiased communication, NASW subscribes to a belief in the importance of avoiding language that might imply sexual, racial, ethnic, or other kinds of discrimination, stereotyping, or bias. NASW is committed to the fair and equal treatment of individuals and groups, and material submitted should not promote stereotypes or discriminatory attitudes and assumptions about people.

Advertising rates are available on request. Publication of an advertisement does not constitute an endorsement or approval of any products or services advertised, any point of view, standard, or opinion presented therein. NASW is not responsible for any claims made in an advertisement appearing in its publications. To advertise, please contact Linda Hann: linda.hann@oup.com. Tel: +44 (0)1367 710022 (please call during UK working hours only).

Published quarterly in February, May, August, and November by the National Association of Social Workers, 750 First Street, NE, Suite 800, Washington, DC 20002-4241.

Print subscription rates: NASW members, $92 for 1 year; NASW student members, $46 for 1 year; nonmembers: individuals, $117 for 1 year; libraries/institutions, $184 for 1 year; corporate, $229 for 1 year. For a print subscription, please contact Oxford Journals at jnlorders@oup.com or 1(800) 852-7323. For online subscription, go to http://naswpress.org/publications/journals/hsw.html

Health & Social Work is indexed/abstracted in *Abstracts in Anthropology; Abstracts in Social Gerontology; Academic Abstracts; AgeLine; Applied Social Sciences Index & Abstracts (ASSIA); caredata, Cumulative Index to Nursing & Allied Health Literature (CINAHL); ERIC/Cass; Exceptional Children Education Resources; Medline; Psychological Abstracts/PsycINFO/PsycLIT; Public Affairs Information Services Bulletin (PAIS); Sage Family Studies Abstracts; Social Sciences Citation Index; Social Sciences Index/Social Sciences Abstracts; Social Work Abstracts; and Sociological Abstracts (SA)/Social Planning, Policy, and Development Abstracts (SOPODA).*

National Headquarters and Publishing Office: National Association of Social Workers, 750 First Street, NE, Suite 800, Washington, DC 20002-4241. Telephone: 202-408-8600, 800-638-8799, TTD 202-336-8396. http://www.naswpress.org

Periodical class mail postage paid at Washington, DC, and at additional mailing offices. Postmaster: Send address changes to Journals Customer Service Department, Oxford University Press, 2001 Evans Road, Cary, NC 27513-2009.

Copyright © 2016 by the National Association of Social Workers, Inc. Produced for NASW Press by Oxford Journals, a division of Oxford University Press. Printed in the United States of America.

February 2016
Volume 41, Number 1
Pages 1–68

HEALTH & SOCIAL WORK

A JOURNAL OF THE NATIONAL ASSOCIATION OF SOCIAL WORKERS
http://www.naswpress.org

TABLE OF CONTENTS

GUEST EDITORIAL

5   Interprofessional Education of Health Professionals: Social Workers Should Lead the Way
Laura D. Taylor, Darla Spence Coffey, and T. Michael Kashner

ARTICLES

9   Engaging Consumer Voices in Health Care Policy: Lessons for Social Work Practice
Kristi Lohmeier Law and Jeanne A. Saunders

17   Parental Leave Policy as a Strategy to Improve Outcomes among Premature Infants
Jennifer C. Greenfield and Susanne Klawetter

25   Female Genital Mutilation Is a Violation of Reproductive Rights of Women: Implications for Health Workers
Suresh Banayya Jungari

33   Impact of Death Work on Self: Existential and Emotional Challenges and Coping of Palliative Care Professionals
Wallace Chi Ho Chan, Agnes Fong, Karen Lok Yi Wong, Doris Man Wah Tse, Kam Shing Lau, and Lai Ngor Chan

42   Traumatic Exposure History as a Risk Factor for Chronic Pain in Adult Patients with Sickle Cell Disease
Teresa Works, Sasia Jones, James Grady, and Biree Andemariam

51   Effectiveness of an Ongoing, Community-Based Breast Cancer Prevention Program for Korean American Women
Eun Koh, Ga-Young Choi, and Ji Young Cho

The following online-only articles are available at http://hsw.oxfordjournals.org/content/current

e1   Substance Use Outcomes of an Integrated HIV–Substance Use Treatment Model Implemented by Social Workers and HIV Medical Providers
Rae Jean Proeschold-Bell, Susan Reif, Baishakhi Taylor, Ashwin Patkar, Paolo Mannelli, Jia Yao, and Evelyn Byrd Quinlivan

e11 Reproductive Coercion by an Intimate Partner: Occurrence, Associations, and Interference with Sexual Health Decision Making
Jonel Thaller and Jill Theresa Messing

e20 Gender and Attitudes about Mental Health Help Seeking: Results from National Data
Douglas Wendt and Kevin Shafer

e29 Exploring Intimate Partner Violence and Sexual Health Needs in the Southwestern United States: Perspectives from Health and Human Services Workers
Eva Margarita Moya, Silvia María Chávez-Baray, Omar Martínez, and Aurora Aguirre-Polanco

e38 Shockingly Uninvolved: Potential for Social Work Practice and Leadership in Implanted Defibrillator Care
Christopher E. Knoepke and Rachel Johnson-Koenke

e44 Health Literacy and Quality of Care among Latino Immigrants in the United States
Rocío Calvo

PRACTICE FORUM

60   Using mHealth in Social Work Practice with Low-Income Hispanic Patients
Joyce Y. Lee and Sri Harathi

BOOK REVIEW

64   *Losing Tim: How Our Health and Education Systems Failed My Son with Schizophrenia*
Paul Gionfriddo
Reviewed by Mandy Ann Fauble

GUEST EDITORIAL

Interprofessional Education of Health Professionals: Social Workers Should Lead the Way

Laura D. Taylor, Darla Spence Coffey, and T. Michael Kashner

There is evidence that when health care professionals work together, patients receive better quality care and better health outcomes (Institute of Medicine [IOM], the National Academies of Sciences, Engineering, and Medicine, 2013). However, preparing practitioners to work collaboratively in teams requires fundamental changes in the way that health care professionals are selected and educated. Many health care settings and health professional educational programs have been creating opportunities for interprofessional education (IPE) to support this team-based care approach. Further research is needed to understand the effects of an interdisciplinary approach on patient outcomes, but there is also a need to understand which professions are poised to adopt this way of practice and why.

Throughout its history, social work has embraced an interdisciplinary philosophy in which interprofessional collaboration is both the bedrock of professional education and the very core of clinical practice. Social work can be found at the intersection of person and environment, in the integration of the biopsychosocial and spiritual aspects of caring for individuals, their families, and the community, and in the operation of micro, mezzo, and macro health systems.

Other health professions have begun to embrace the concept of interprofessional teams by focusing on education. IPE is defined in a recent IOM report as occurring "when learners of two or more health and/or social care professions engage in learning with, from, and about each other to improve collaboration and the delivery of care" (IOM, the National Academies of Sciences, Engineering, and Medicine, 2015, p. xi). A fundamental aspect of social work education includes preparing trainees for practice in host agencies. However, according to the 2013 Annual Statistics on Social Work Education collected by the Council on Social Work Education (2014), approximately 25 percent of BSW and 44 percent of MSW programs specifically include IPE components. This is quite significant given that there are nearly 750 accredited social work degree programs (506 BSW and 238 MSW programs). Woven throughout the social work curriculum is an expectation that social workers will eventually practice in agencies representing a diversity of professions who are critical in addressing the social needs of our most vulnerable citizens.

Social work has long recognized the professional skills necessary to create effective members of interprofessional teams, including, but not limited to, effective communication, collaborative problem solving, patient- or person-centered care, systems thinking, and the practice of "starting where the client is." In addition, much of what is considered good interprofessional practice has long been standard social work practice in areas such as case management, palliative care, oncology, work with veterans, school social work, child welfare services, and child and adolescent mental health treatment, to name a few.

According to Bronstein (2003), "interdisciplinary collaboration is the achievement of goals that cannot be reached when individual professions act on their own" (p. 299). For social workers, learning to practice collaboratively may be less of an innovation and more of the linchpin of team-based care that connects the system of care with the clients receiving services and their families. Other clinical health professions have embraced the importance of IPE. However, it remains to be seen whether those in training value the importance of IPE as part of their learning to become health professionals and whether IPE even improves interprofessional practice and collaborative behaviors.

There is evidence from the U.S. Department of Veterans Affairs (VA) as to the extent different health profession trainees value the importance of learning interprofessional care as part of their overall clinical learning experience. The VA has a long history of interprofessional clinical training of physicians, nurses, social workers, psychologists, and many others. Since 2001, the Veterans Health Administration's Office of Academic Affiliations (OAA) has assessed the VA clinical training experience by administering annually to all of its trainees the anonymous, voluntary, nationwide, centrally administered, Web-based Learners' Perceptions Survey (Kashner, Bernett, & Wicker, 2015; Keitz, Holland, Melander, Bosworth, & Pincus, 2003). Respondent trainees representing essentially all health professions are asked to rate their satisfaction on a five-item Likert scale for each of 15 elements describing different aspects of VA's clinical learning environment, plus a summary question that rates their overall clinical learning experiences with VA. The 15 element responses are consistent (Cronbach's alpha = .96) and one-dimensional (second highest eigenvalue = 0.87 < 1).

Rather than asking trainees to tell us directly what elements they valued most in driving their overall satisfaction with the clinical learning environments, OAA inferred such preferences by calculating how a trainee's satisfaction with each element independently correlated with his or her overall satisfaction with the clinical learning environment (Kashner, Hettler, et al., 2015). Analysis revealed that universally, across all professions, quality of care was most highly correlated with overall satisfaction. On the other hand, there were distinct differences among professions in how ratings for interdisciplinary approach to care contributed to overall satisfaction. To assess trainee preferences for IPE, we computed a "preference index" by dividing the strength of the association between interdisciplinary approach and overall satisfaction by the strength of the association between quality of care and overall satisfaction. Thus, an index of 50 percent means that trainees value the importance of IPE at 50 percent of how they value quality of care for their clinical learning environment.

Table 1 shows both the preference index for interprofessional care learning and its rank among the 15 elements that make up the clinical learning environment. Notice that a profession can place high

Table 1: Preference Index Scores Assessing How Trainees Valued Interprofessional Team Care Based on Rating Their VA Clinical Learning Environment Experiences, by Professional Discipline

Profession or Discipline	Sample Size (n)	Preference Index[a] (%)	95% Confidence Interval	Rank[b]
Social work	3,569	59.7	43.3, 76.2	3
Rehabilitation	2,402	59.1	39.6, 78.6	3
Technician	2,028	57.1	33.1, 81.0	3
Psychology	3,435	53.3	39.5, 67.0	4
Pharmacy	7,780	51.9	39.1, 64.7	6
Optometry	2,129	44.9	23.5, 66.2	7
Dietitian	1,221	43.3	−20.4, 107.1	8
Dentistry	1,968	35.0	13.1, 56.7	13
Audiology and speech pathology	1,187	32.7	1.6, 63.8	13
Nursing	41,005	29.8	24.0, 35.5	15
Physician assistant	1,199	29.6	3.9, 55.4	14
Podiatry	1,017	26.9	3.9, 49.9	14
Surgery	6,339	22.9	14.0, 31.9	14
Medical student	16,409	21.2	14.7, 27.7	14
Hospital-based medicine	3,615	17.7	5.2, 30.1	14
Medicine subspecialties	3,899	16.5	4.3, 28.6	14
Other medicine	4,608	12.0	1.3, 22.8	15
Internal medicine	14,060	10.8	4.7, 16.9	15
Psychiatry	3,717	8.0	−3.8, 19.7	15

Note: VA = U.S. Department of Veterans Affairs.
[a]Index preference scores reflect the extent to which satisfaction with interprofessional team care drives overall satisfaction with the clinical learning environment measured as a percentage that satisfaction with quality of care also drives overall satisfaction with the clinical learning environment.
[b]Ranking the size by which interprofessional team care rating drives overall rating of the clinical learning environment among the effect sizes to all 15 elements that make up the clinical learning environment domain: time working with patients, degree of supervision, degree of autonomy, amount of noneducational "scut" work, interdisciplinary approach, prep for clinical practice, prep for future training, prep for business aspects of clinical practice, time for learning, access to specialty expertise, teaching conferences, quality of care, culture of patient safety, spectrum of patient problems, and diversity of patients.

value on learning interprofessional care even though as an element, it ranks near the bottom among all elements within the clinical learning environment.

Both in terms of an overall preference score and how it ranked among other elements, social work trainees tended to value IPE highest among all health professions, followed closely by rehabilitation, technicians, psychology, and pharmacy. At the other end of the spectrum, psychiatry, internal medicine, and other medicine residents placed a much lower value on IPE, both in terms of an overall score and how they ranked IPE among other elements. This ranking has significance in terms of advancing IPE and collaborative practice. Despite their interest in IPE over the past two decades, physician residents generally, and internal medicine specifically, are among the health trainees with the lowest index scores.

Nursing appears in the middle, above physicians but below other nonphysician professions. These data reflect the success social work has had on emphasizing for its student trainees the importance of interprofessional teams in caring for patients. Despite this obvious success, social work programs are often overlooked as models when curricula are designed to train the other health professions to work cooperatively to benefit patient care.

We believe how social work trainees rank the importance of IPE suggests that social work education and the social work profession offer effective models that other professions may use to improve the preparation of interprofessional collaboration. So, what underlies social work success in selecting students and conveying to them the value of interprofessional team care? It may be that because social work practice often occurs within "host" settings (within health, education, and justice systems, for example), there is a fundamental emphasis in its education and training to be team-oriented and boundary-spanning that lends itself to intuitive interprofessional and collaborative practice. To better understand such characteristics and the apparent foundational attributes of IPE in social work training programs, it is important to understand the inherent values of an interprofessional approach to practice and policy development.

Seeking the input and engagement from multiple professions strengthens a variety of core elements in care delivery, including, but not limited to, differing insights of the problems or solutions, consideration of varied perspectives in addressing patient needs or challenges, and using the diversity of interprofessional approaches to create a more comprehensive framework to health care delivery. A single perspective or approach can have limitations and neglect the complexities and alternatives that are inherent in being human.

Social work has long incorporated an interdisciplinary viewpoint in which collaboration with other professions is central to both the foundation of professional education and a fundamental part of clinical practice. From these data, we contend that social work education may very well teach the importance of an interprofessional approach to health care delivery. With a person-in-environment perspective, social work's commitment to understanding the biopsychosocial and spiritual aspects of individuals, their families, and the community is threaded through those entering social work, the delivery of clinical practice, and the philosophical approach to program development in health care settings. We thus strongly believe that social work is well positioned to take a leadership role in paving the way for successful implementation of IPE in other health professions. HSW

REFERENCES

Bronstein, L. R. (2003). A model for interdisciplinary collaboration. *Social Work, 48*, 297–306.

Council on Social Work Education. (2014). *2013 statistics on social work education in the United States*. Retrieved from http://www.cswe.org/File.aspx?id=74478

Institute of Medicine, the National Academies of Sciences, Engineering, and Medicine. (2013). *Global forum on innovation in health professional education: Learning how to improve health from interprofessional models across the continuum of education to practice: Workshop summary*. Retrieved from http://iom.nationalacademies.org/Reports/2013/Interprofessional-Education-for-Collaboration.aspx

Institute of Medicine, the National Academies of Sciences, Engineering, and Medicine. (2015). *Measuring the impact of interprofessional education on collaborative practice and patient outcomes*. Retrieved from http://books.nap.edu/openbook.php?record_id=21726

Kashner, T. M., Bernett, D. S., & Wicker, A. B. (2015). *Learners' Perceptions Survey: Instructions manual for data users*. Washington, DC: Office of Academic Affiliations.

Kashner, T. M., Hettler, D. L., Zeiss, R. A., Aron, D. C., Bernett, D. S., Brannen, J. L., et al. (2015). *Has interprofessional education changed learning preferences? A national perspective*. Unpublished manuscript, U.S. Department of Veterans Affairs.

Keitz, S. A., Holland, G. J., Melander, E. H., Bosworth, H. B., & Pincus, S. H. (2003). The Veterans Affairs Learners' Perceptions Survey: The foundation for education quality improvement. *Academic Medicine, 78*, 910–917.

Laura D. Taylor, LSCSW, *is national director of social work, care management and social work services, U.S. Department of Veterans Affairs (VA), 810 Vermont Avenue, NW (10P4C), Washington, DC 20420, e-mail: laura.taylor@va.gov.*

Darla Spence Coffey, PhD, MSW, is president and chief executive officer, Council on Social Work Education, Alexandria, VA. *T. Michael Kashner, PhD, JD,* is health science specialist, Office of Academic Affiliations, VA, Washington, DC, and associate vice chair for education research and research professor of medicine, Loma Linda University Medical School, Loma Linda, CA. All statements and descriptions expressed herein do not necessarily reflect the opinions or positions of the VA or its affiliated institutions, or of the Council on Social Work Education.

Advance Access Publication December 8, 2015

PRACTICE FORUM

Have you worked with a practice innovation readers should know about? The Practice Forum editor can help you develop your insights into an article for this column. Describe your innovation in eight double-spaced pages or fewer and send as a Word document through the online portal at http://hsw.msubmit.net (initial, one-time registration is required).

READERS: WRITE TO US!

Submit your reactions to and comments about an article published in *Health & Social Work* or a contemporary issue in the field. Send your letter (three double-spaced pages or fewer) as a Word document through the online portal at http://hsw.msubmit.net (initial, one-time registration is required).

NASW PRESS POLICY ON ETHICAL BEHAVIOR

The NASW Press expects authors to adhere to ethical standards for scholarship as articulated in the NASW *Code of Ethics* and *Writing for the NASW Press: Information for Authors.* These standards include actions such as

- taking responsibility and credit only for work they have actually performed
- honestly acknowledging the work of others
- submitting only original work to journals
- fully documenting their own and others' related work.

If possible breaches of ethical standards have been identified at the review or publication process, the NASW Press may notify the author and bring the ethics issue to the attention of the appropriate professional body or other authority. Peer review confidentiality will not apply where there is evidence of plagiarism.

As reviewed and revised by
NASW National Committee on
Inquiry (NCOI), May 30, 1997

Approved by NASW Board of
Directors, September 1997

Engaging Consumer Voices in Health Care Policy: Lessons for Social Work Practice

Kristi Lohmeier Law and Jeanne A. Saunders

Community health centers provide comprehensive public health care in some of the most disadvantaged communities in the United States. To ensure that health centers meet the needs of their consumers, they uniquely engage them in their organizational decision-making and policy-development processes by requiring that their boards of directors encompass a 51 percent consumer majority. To understand the quality of board members' experiences, a critical ethnography was conducted using Arnstein's ladder of citizen participation and the socioecological model as a framework. The analysis identified multiple influences on the quality of participation among consumer members. Findings also confirm other research that has found that knowledge of the economic, political, and cultural factors surrounding the context of the individual health center is important to understanding meaningful participation. The experience is important to understand given the shift driven by the Patient Protection and Affordable Care Act of 2010 in health care, which emphasizes a patient-centered model of care. Social work practitioners and others in the public health arena interested in empowering consumers to have a role in the provision of services need to understand the impact of each of these areas and the experience of this unique sample of health center board members.

KEY WORDS: *advocacy; consumer engagement; patient-centered care; Patient Protection and Affordable Care Act of 2010; public health policy development*

Media messages about the passage and implementation of the Patient Protection and Affordable Care Act of 2010 (ACA) (P.L. 111-148) focused on the role of the individual as a consumer in the health care system. Provisions in the ACA that have received less media attention are those that provide increased funding for federally funded community health centers (hereafter health centers), which typically serve low-income individuals (Iglehart, 2010). The ACA established the Community Health Center Fund to provide $11 billion over a five-year period to be distributed to health centers across the country (Health Resources and Services Administration [HRSA], 2014).

Health centers (also known as federally qualified health centers, or FQHCs) were first created under the 1964 Economic Opportunity Act (EOA). They typically are located in areas with large populations living at or near the poverty line and (historically) uninsured, but they serve all people regardless of income or insurance status. To meet the comprehensive health care needs of the community in which they are located, health centers employ an array of professionals, such as nurses, primary care physicians, pharmacists, social workers, accountants, and others. A unique feature of these health centers is that their boards of directors are mandated to have a consumer majority (51 percent) (National Association of Community Health Centers, 2011). The consumer-participation requirement was suggested for a number of programs created by the EOA to ensure that the consumers who receive services are involved in the development and implementation of programs created to meet their needs (Reisch & Andrews, 2001); however, the 51 percent consumer majority was only mandated for health centers. In the context of health centers, a *consumer* is defined by the HRSA, which oversees the health centers, as a patient who uses the clinic services for his or her usual source of care, often used once within a two-year period (NACHC, 2011).

The expansion of the health centers under the ACA, together with the consumer-majority mandate, provides a unique opportunity for some individuals from disadvantaged communities to be actively engaged in their communities by serving on the board of directors. This is a unique form of citizen participation that allows individuals to be actively involved in the development and implementation of health policy. Having this opportunity to influence policy at a level that affects many in the community is much different than making personal or family decisions about health care.

The qualitative study reported here was conducted to better understand to what degree consumer representatives on health center boards play a vital role in the development and implementation of policies that guide the provision of health care services in their communities—that is, to better understand the "quality" of the consumers' participation on these boards.

LITERATURE REVIEW
Citizen Participation

A clear distinction exists in the literature on citizen participation between quantifying participation and the quality of that participation. Research has quantified citizen participation in multiple contexts as a count of the activities and behaviors that involve nonelected citizens contributing to policy-development processes (see, for example, Alex-Assensoh, 1997; Brady, Verba, & Scholzman, 1995; Casciano, 2007; Lelieveldt, 2004; Swaroop & Morenoff, 2006; Wang, 2001; Zimmerman & Rappaport, 1988). This literature suggests that despite existing barriers to participation, which include individual characteristics (for example, education or income levels) (Brady et al., 1995; Ritter, 2008) and contextual characteristics (for example, neighborhood poverty or racial and ethnic composition) (Casciano, 2007; Houston & Ong, 2011), nonelected citizens are participating in quantifiable activities such as voting, attending neighborhood association meetings, and discussing issues of importance with local and state elected officials to create policy change. This, however, is not the whole story, for the number of participants attending an event, for example, does not address the quality of their input or the value placed on their opinions or experiences. It is this focus on the quality of participation that was examined in this study.

During the creation and implementation of the War on Poverty legislation during the 1960s, social justice advocates, organizers, and scholars began to pay closer attention not only to the question of how many voices were involved or heard in decision-making processes, but also to the legitimacy with which they were heard. It was in this context that Arnstein (1969) developed a lens through which to critique the quality of citizen participation. Arnstein used an eight-rung ladder to depict a continuum of participation, beginning with nonparticipation on the lowest rung and rising to full citizen control at the highest rung. The principal investigator (PI) of the current study expanded on this model to include an interpretation of how the power or legitimate voice of consumers increases with rising levels of quality participation (Law, 2013). For this interpretation, at the lowest rung of the ladder consumers have little power over policy development and implementation, but at the highest level the consumers' voice is legitimized as the power is distributed into the hands of many (Law, 2013).

Health Center Boards of Directors: Consumers' Role

Health centers in the United States have three simultaneous goals: (1) to serve the underserved, (2) to respond to community needs, and (3) to ensure consumer majority governance (Geiger, 2005). HRSA, which is charged with ensuring that health centers remain in compliance with federal policy (Section 330 of the Public Health Service Act [42 U.S.C. § 254b]; see HRSA, 2012), provides further guidance for health centers. This section specifically notes that consumer members provide their expertise to board decisions similar to the way others with more technical expertise lend their voices.

There is a dearth of literature on the quality of consumers' participation on health center boards, especially from the board members' perspective. However, Wright (2013) examined the income and education levels of more than 2,000 health center board members and concluded that some consumers are "more representative" of the client population than others. He suggested there should be a distinction made between "representative" and "nonrepresentative" consumers based on their income, education level, and professional status. In fact, Wright questioned whether nonrepresentative consumers (those with incomes, education, and so on higher than the typical client population) should even be counted in the consumer-representative majority.

Given that there is little research on the quality of consumers' participation on health center boards and with the changing health care environment potentially allowing for greater consumer participation in the future, the present study was conducted in a midwestern state to answer the research question,

"How do community health center boards facilitate the quality of citizen participation in policy development?"

METHOD
Critical Ethnography

Carspecken's (1996) model for conducting a critical ethnography guided the conduct of this study. The purpose of a critical ethnography is "to understand the relationship of culture to social structures" (Hardcastle, Usher, & Holmes, 2006, p. 152) by reconstructing a social reality by privileging multiple voices in that reconstruction (Carspecken, 1996). There are five phases of inquiry and process in a critical ethnography: (1) *monological data collection*, objectively collected primary data defined as "what is and what takes place" in a contextual setting (health center boards in this study; examples of monological data collected in it include board meeting minutes for one calendar year and data from interviews with national- and state-level policy experts about the history, structure, and operations of health centers); (2) *preliminary reconstructive analysis*, which examines the primary (monological) data to infer meaning; (3) *dialogical data generation*, which incorporates findings from the first two phases and uses it to inform the interviews with participants in the study's social site context; (4) *description of system relationships* between the social site and social groups; and (5) *explaining system relationships* within the broad views of society (Carspecken & Apple, 1992). This article focuses on the results from the first three phases of this model.

Socioecological Perspective

To fit with Carspecken's model, a multidimensional view was necessary to understand the many influences on board members' quality of participation. McLeroy, Bibeau, Steckler, and Glanz (1988) proposed a socioecological perspective, a modified version of Bronfenbrenner's (1979) ecological perspective, which was used to create the interview guide and conduct the data analysis. McLeroy and colleagues used this perspective to examine public policy, political power, and its individual impact on individuals within a particular context from multiple levels. The socioecological perspective includes factors at five levels of influence: intrapersonal, interpersonal, organizational or institutional, community, and public policy. Each level is briefly described in the context of this study. The connections within the socioecological perspective provided a suitable prism to investigate the ways these multiple levels of an individual's life might affect the quality of his or her participation.

Sample Selection and Description of Participants

All procedures were approved by a university review board prior to the conduct of the study. All participants were assured of their confidentiality and that identifying information related to the board they served on, its location, and so forth would not be identified in any report.

The three health center boards in a midwestern state and their attendant clinics included in this study were identified with the assistance of the state's primary care association (PCA). Criteria used to select these boards included having an active board with a regular meeting schedule and diversity in geographic location to ensure that boards from different areas of the state would be represented. Each of the boards selected had 12 to 15 members, and the clinic director served in an ex officio capacity. Following suggestions of the PCA, the clinic director and board chair were contacted by the PI and arrangements were made to attend a board meeting to explain the study. All board members were provided an information sheet about the study and the PI's contact information. People interested in participating in the study were asked to contact the PI to schedule an interview.

A total of 16 (of the possible 45) board members representing each of the three boards agreed to participate and subsequently scheduled and completed an interview. The typical participant was a white man, between the ages of 46 and 64. (A complete description of the participants can be found at http://ir.uiowa.edu/cgi/viewcontent.cgi?article=4687&context=etd.) Eight of the participants identified themselves as meeting the definition of a consumer, six as representative consumer, and two as nonrepresentative consumer board members, following Wright's (2013) definitions. Board members were currently working in or had retired from a diverse array of professions. They also had a wide array of volunteer experiences serving their communities or within their places of worship.

Data Collection

Semistructured interviews were conducted with each participant and typically lasted from 60 to 90 minutes. The number of participants and the length of the interviews met the criteria for theoretical saturation (Creswell, 2007). The wording of questions was changed slightly during each interview to reflect the role of the interviewee. For example, when talking with a nonconsumer-representative board member, the questions asked were, "How would you describe your role and contribution on the board?" and "How do you see the role played by the consumer representatives on this board?" A similar question to a consumer representative board member was worded as, "How do you see your role as a consumer representative on this board?" Probing questions were used to invite the participants to add additional comments or provide concrete examples of their experiences. All interviews were digitally recorded and transcribed as they occurred, which allowed for the recursive process of the data collected to inform future interviews and theoretical and conceptual saturation processes.

Data Analysis

All phases of the data analysis were conducted using NVivo 9 (QSR International, 2011). Initial coding of the data was conducted following Carspecken's (1996) model, which uses low-level coding and horizon analysis. The goal of these types of inferences is for the researcher "to put more words onto the actions observed, as if the actor had tried to convey the entire meaning of her act verbally rather than through the complexities of vocal tone, posture, gesture, facial expression, timing, prosodic form, and so on" (Carspecken, 1996, p. 97). To increase the rigor of the analysis, two members of the research team who did not participate in the interviews reviewed all coding. The few differences between coders were resolved on an individual basis. Member checking was also used to ensure the accuracy of meaning represented by the participants' comments. Twelve of the 16 participants agreed to take part in the member checking process.

RESULTS

As noted, the socioecological perspective provided the framework for analysis in this study, and the results are presented below within these levels of influence. Participants talked about their personal experiences at each level, as well as their observations of the board members as a whole.

Intrapersonal-Level Factors Influencing Participation

Intrapersonal level factors influencing citizen participation include resources such as knowledge and skills that the individual possesses and characteristics of the individual's identity, such as race or ethnicity, gender, age, and socioeconomic status (McLeroy et al., 1988). Some of these individual characteristics were viewed as beneficial to increasing participation, and others were viewed more as a detriment. All of the participants recognized how their own and others' education and work experiences increased the quality of their participation. With respect to consumer-representative board members, many participants noted that consumer members with higher educational backgrounds or more professional work experience—for example, as an accountant—brought multiple dimensions to their consumer participation, which was viewed favorably. A representative consumer member employed in a helping profession stated,

> But then I'm also [a helping professional] who does frontline [work], and a lot of the people I deal with everyday also go to the [clinic]. So, I think what I bring to the table is a little bit different perspective than a lot, even some of the other consumer board members, because they are not also [in the helping profession].

Some participants believed that a lack of education or professional work experience put board members (in particular, consumer representatives) at a disadvantage and reduced the quality of their participation. For example, one nonconsumer participant referred to this barrier when he described the complicated nature of the financial terms with which the health center boards must be familiar to provide accountability to the health center's finances and recognized that it was difficult for "everyone" to understand the nuances and complexity involved. One representative consumer participant articulated his personal feelings of inadequacy:

> Right now I think we have a really good balance of people with good education and experiences, and I feel lately I have felt very inadequate to be on the board or around all these people that are so educated but—and I have to tell myself something—I have [a] right to be on that board, and if they don't want me to, they have the right to ask me to leave.

In contrast, one representative consumer board member on a different board with little work or educational experience was not only viewed as unique, but in different interviews was also referred to as a "voice of reason" during discussions at board meetings. This individual represented the large number of patients with a particular (social) characteristic served by the clinic.

For some, personal characteristics were a hindrance to greater participation. For example, a representative consumer member with a particular health condition often treated at the health center found this health issue to limit her ability to regularly attend meetings and participate more fully. Other individual characteristics of participants, such as race or ethnicity, were not specifically identified as influencing the quality of participation by board members.

Interpersonal-Level Factors Influencing Participation

The interpersonal level of the socioecological perspective refers to the influence of relationships on participation (McLeroy et al., 1988), such as the relationships of individuals with family members, friends, neighbors, work colleagues, or other acquaintances. The interpersonal level in this study focused on the relationships between the health center board members, between board members and board chairs, between board chairs and clinic directors, and between the board and the leadership or management team of the clinics. The themes that emerged within this level included two sets of relationships that influenced board members' participation: those between the board members and the leadership or management team of the clinics and those between the board members and the board chairs. These relationships were identified as having the most influence on the quality of the consumer board members' participation because of the way they facilitated their ability to legitimately participate.

First, across all interviews, the relationship and trust between the clinic's leadership or management team and the members of the board facilitated and even enhanced the participation of all members. Consumer (both representative and nonrepresentative) and nonconsumer members alike identified these relationships as important to the quality of participation for board members. For example, a nonconsumer member described the way a leadership team member assisted in her understanding of the financial issues addressed by the board: "And [the finance director], any time [I] got a question; [he] is very good at explaining [it] and breaking it down."

The second theme, the relationship between the board members and the board chair, was identified as facilitating the quality of participation of consumer members in particular. For example, one representative consumer member, a former board chair, described her strategy to ensure that voice was given specifically to consumer members on the board: an open agenda time incorporated into board meetings when all members had the opportunity to make a comment, ask a question, or in another way be heard in the context of the health center board environment. In another example, a clinic director observed that a board chair, given his leadership position, played a key role in drawing out the perspectives of consumer members during discussions.

In addition, multiple board members across all three sites identified the importance of the collective roles of each board member in fulfilling the responsibilities of the health center boards. They recognized that, to make the best decisions possible to meet the needs of consumers, the board as a whole (that is, all members) must participate. A representative consumer member described this importance: "They [all board members] all put forth their own aspect on it so that ... each view is different. ... We all kind of put a little niche into it so ... it takes all of us to make a full decision on it."

Organizational- or Institutional-Level Factors Influencing Participation

The next level of the socioecological framework focuses on how the organization or institutional structures of health center boards influenced board members' ability to have a quality participation experience on the board. The two structures identified were the leadership or management teams of the clinics and the organizational and institutional support provided by the National Association of Community Health Centers (NACHC) and the PCA. For board members who did not have expertise in policy and health care advocacy, these entities provided crucial support and education about their roles as advocates for the health center and health policy and about the policy-development process in general. One nonconsumer board member described the support received from the PCA as facilitating the board's ability to affect government policy:

> Collectively through the board association [PCA]—that's how it [our board] may contribute to the development of policy, I mean, government policy. I think that having our voice in the state capitol and having a voice out in Washington collectively, that's how the board contributes [to policy].

Another nonrepresentative consumer member discussed the role of the NACHC in helping the board understand the efforts and challenges of health centers of similar size in other areas of the country and sometimes connecting them directly to those boards, thereby improving his or her work on the board. Other participants described the clinic director's role in facilitating this information flow:

> I know that [our clinic director] is very good about taking people on the board to national meetings particularly in Washington [with the NACHC], so that they are exposed to the advocacy piece where they actually get to meet with our representatives and tell the story of the community health center.

Community-Level Factors Influencing Participation

According to McLeroy et al. (1988), the community-level influence on citizen participation involves a political entity with one or more structures of power, such as local, state, or federal decision makers. Participants believed that informal and formal relationships between board members and clinic staff with local, state, or federal policymakers were vital to the survival and growth of the health centers. Board members reported their typical contact with policymakers was limited to a "day on the Hill" with legislators that was organized by the PCA. However, universally the clinic director and the PCA were identified as having the most direct contact with policymakers at every level. It was when the clinic director or the PCA shared their interactions with the board members that the quality of participation was most affected. This shared information propelled knowledge acquisition for all board members about issues, advocacy strategies, and members' advocacy roles, which collectively increased the quality of participation. The increase in quality was believed to apply to all board members, not just the consumer members.

Public Policy–Level Factors Influencing Participation

The focus of this level of influence in the socioecological model is on how public policy affects the quality of consumer members' participation on the board. Two policies were consistently identified: the 51 percent consumer majority on the boards (having the most direct impact on ensuring the presence of consumers on the board but not addressing the quality of their participation) and the way the ACA affects the consumer members' participation. The impact of the ACA was more covert. Although not always directly addressed during interviews, the PI observed board meeting discussions that explored possible changes from implementation of the ACA that could affect consumers' participation on the boards. For example, the ACA increased funding to health centers so they could serve more patients, and it was discussed that more of these new patients would likely be middle-class people looking for a health care home. This new patient population was believed to be in direct contrast to the traditional consumer (that is, having a low income and being uninsured and of diverse backgrounds). Potentially, consumer representatives would no longer represent the consumers for which the health centers were first established.

DISCUSSION

This study examined multiple influences on the quality of consumers' participation on health center boards in a midwestern state. Health center boards provided a unique setting to examine the quality of consumers' participation because they are mandated to have a 51 percent majority of consumer representatives, thereby guaranteeing the potential sample. By looking at the multiple levels of influence described in the socioecological perspective (McLeroy et al., 1988), this study was better able to identify the complexity and interrelatedness of multiple influences on consumers having a legitimate voice in policy development on health center boards. Too often it appears that the quality of consumers' participation is evaluated on the basis of personal characteristics only. The results suggest that, in fact, all five levels of influence examined play a critical role in the ability of consumers to contribute in a meaningful way.

Using Arnstein's (1969) ladder of citizen participation, one can see the extent to which the health center boards facilitate a quality citizen-participation experience for their consumer board members. First, Arnstein's ladder questioned whether those traditionally absent from decision-making processes could enjoy legitimate voice simply by having a seat at the decision-making table. In other words, was it enough to include them in the process to ensure their legitimate or quality participation? The results of this study suggest it does not. Although numerous board members discussed the individual power of consumer members through their existence on the board, it was not at all clear that this translated into the collective power that comes with representativeness. This collective power seems more in line with the spirit of the 51 percent consumer majority. The question raised by this distinction suggests that more research in this area is crucial to understanding its complexity.

Second, although there was the collective recognition by all participants that consumer perspectives were valued on the board, they were not viewed as more important than their nonconsumer counterparts', which seems counter to the spirit of the 51 percent consumer majority on health center boards. Arnstein's ultimate goal of citizen control suggests that consumer perspective is privileged when it comes to decision-making processes about the services consumers receive, which directly affects their life quality and well-being, such as health care–related services.

Limitations and Future Research Considerations

As with any study, limitations are present in this study. The study used a small sample size and was limited geographically. The participants represented slightly less than 40 percent of the total potential sample, which was adequate for this qualitative study and allowed for saturation of responses. However, it is possible that these were also the most engaged board members (consumers and nonconsumers), and thus their comments are not representative of the others who chose not to participate. In addition, the boards that were selected for the study were among the most active boards in one state. It is not clear from this study how the experience of these board members, and the boards as a whole, might differ from those of less active boards or boards in other states. Similarly, each state has a primary care association that would have a relationship to the boards in that state. This relationship would be different between each PCA and each board in every state, thereby changing aspects of the results depending on the relationships. The role of the PCAs would be another area of inquiry to pursue in future research.

Although a strength of this study is that it examined consumer participation from multiple levels using the socioecological perspective, it is important to recognize that using other theoretical models could provide additional information that would be useful in understanding ways to increase the participation of consumers. One significant question that should be addressed in future research is how does one measure the quality of citizen participation in contexts where consumers are required to participate? To answer this question from a social justice perspective, future research should engage consumers participating in these policy-development decision-making processes as active participants in the research. A community-based participation research method could be used to understand the complexity of this experience from the viewpoint provided by those living and breathing it every day.

CONCLUSION

Social work is uniquely positioned in multiple agencies to incorporate consumer voices into discussions about service delivery and other policy decision-making processes. From the results of this study, it is clear that just mandating consumers to take part in policy development (as in the 51 percent majority of health center boards) does not guarantee that their voice is honored in these processes. Social workers bring an array of knowledge and skills to their positions that can be applied to empowering consumers of health care or other services to have a legitimate voice in policy decisions. They also bring a person-in-environment perspective that promotes an understanding of people as part of a dynamic system. Whereas it is easy to dismiss "poor" participation by a consumer member as a personal deficit, the results of this study suggest that individual characteristics are only one influence among others of equal importance. The analysis and results of this study provide a clear example of the multiple influences (the total environment) that can affect an individual's participation on a health center board of directors. Social workers can use their knowledge and skills to help individuals prepare to serve on these boards by understanding the culture and structure of the boards and educating potential participants. Social workers can also focus on the group process within a board and educate members about group dynamics, diversity, bias, and related topics. In addition, social workers have the skills to facilitate collaboration at multiple levels, which strengthens policy change. **HSW**

REFERENCES

Alex-Assensoh, Y. (1997). Race, concentrated poverty, social isolation, and political behavior. *Urban Affairs Review, 33*(2), 209–227.

Arnstein, S. R. (1969). A ladder of citizen participation. *Journal of the American Planning Association, 35*(4), 216–224.

Brady, H. E., Verba, S., & Scholzman, K. L. (1995). Beyond SES: A resource model of political participation. *American Political Science Review, 89*(2), 271–294.

Bronfenbrenner, U. (1979). *The ecology of human development: Experiments by nature and design.* Cambridge, MA: Harvard University Press.

Carspecken, P. F. (1996). *Critical ethnography in educational research: A theoretical and practical guide.* New York: Routledge.

Carspecken, P. F., & Apple, M. (1992). Critical qualitative research: Theory, methodology, and practice. In M. L. LeCompte, W. L. Millroy, & J. Preissle (Eds.), *The handbook of qualitative research in education* (pp. 507–553). San Diego: Academic Press.

Casciano, R. (2007). Political and civic participation among disadvantaged urban mothers: The role of neighborhood poverty. *Social Science Quarterly, 88*, 1124–1151.

Creswell, J. W. (2007). *Qualitative inquiry and research design: Choosing among five approaches.* Thousand Oaks, CA: Sage Publications.

Geiger, H. J. (2005). The first community health centers: A model of enduring value. *Journal of Ambulatory Care Management, 28*, 313–320.

Hardcastle, M., Usher, K., & Holmes, C. (2006). Carspecken's five-stage critical qualitative research method: An application to nursing research. *Qualitative Health Research, 16*(1), 151–161.

Health Resources and Services Administration. (2012). *Health center program requirements.* Retrieved from http://bphc.hrsa.gov/about/requirements/index.html

Health Resources and Services Administration. (2014). *Fact sheet.* Retrieved from http://bphc.hrsa.gov/about/healthcenterfactsheet.pdf

Houston, D., & Ong, P. M. (2011). Determinants of voter participation in neighborhood council elections. *Nonprofit and Voluntary Sector Quarterly, 41*, 686–703.

Iglehart, J. K. (2010). Health centers fill critical gap, enjoy support. *Health Affairs, 29*, 343–345.

Law, K. L. (2013). *An exploration of the quality of citizen participation: Consumer majority boards of community health centers in Iowa.* Unpublished doctoral dissertation, University of Iowa.

Lelieveldt, H. (2004). Helping citizens help themselves: Neighborhood improvement programs and the impact of social networks, trust, and norms on neighborhood-oriented forms of participation. *Urban Affairs Review, 39*, 531–551.

McLeroy, K. R., Bibeau, D., Steckler, A., & Glanz, K. (1988). An ecological perspective on health promotion programs. *Health Education Behavior, 15*, 351–377.

National Association of Community Health Centers. (2011). *So you want to start a health center . . . ?* Retrieved from http://www.nachc.com/client/documents/So20you20want20to20Start-Final20July202011.pdf

Patient Protection and Affordable Care Act, P.L. 111-148, 124 Stat. 119 (March 23, 2010).

QSR International. (2011). NVivo 9 [Computer software]. Burlington, MA: Author.

Reisch, M., & Andrews, J. (2001). *The road not taken: A history of radical social work in the United States.* Philadelphia: Brunner-Routledge.

Ritter, J. A. (2008). A national study predicting licensed social workers' levels of political participation: The role of resources, psychological engagement, and recruitment networks. *Social Work, 53*, 347–357.

Swaroop, S., & Morenoff, J. D. (2006). Building community: The neighborhood context of social organization. *Social Forces, 84*, 1665–1695.

Wang, X. (2001). Assessing public participation in U.S. cities. *Public Performance and Management Review, 24*(4), 322–336.

Wright, B. (2013). Who governs federally qualified health centers? *Journal of Health Politics, Policy and Law, 38*(1), 27–55.

Zimmerman, M. A., & Rappaport, J. (1988). Citizen participation, perceived control, and psychological empowerment. *American Journal of Community Psychology, 16*, 725–750.

Kristi Lohmeier Law, PhD, *is assistant professor of social work, University of Wisconsin–Whitewater, 800 W. Main Street, 5210 Laurentide Hall, Whitewater, WI 53190; e-mail: lawk@uww.edu.* ***Jeanne A. Saunders, PhD, MSSW,*** *is associate professor, School of Social Work, University of Iowa, Iowa City.*

Original manuscript received September 2, 2014
Accepted December 9, 2014
Advance Access Publication December 13, 2015

Parental Leave Policy as a Strategy to Improve Outcomes among Premature Infants

Jennifer C. Greenfield and Susanne Klawetter

Although gains have been made in premature birth rates among racial and ethnic minority and low socioeconomic status populations, tremendous disparities still exist in both prematurity rates and health outcomes for preterm infants. Parental involvement is known to improve health outcomes for preterm babies. However, a gap in evidence exists around whether parental involvement can help ameliorate the disparities in both short- and long-term outcomes for their preterm children. Families more likely to experience preterm birth are also less likely to have access to paid leave and thus experience significant systemic barriers to involvement, especially when their newborns are hospitalized. This article describes the research gap in this area and explores pathways by which social workers may ameliorate disparities in preterm birth outcomes through practice, policy, and research.

KEY WORDS: *Family and Medical Leave Act; health disparities; neonatal intensive care units; parental leave; preterm birth*

Preterm birth in the United States has been the subject of much attention, both as a public health issue and as an example of the pervasive health disparities that continue to affect certain racial and ethnic minority populations (American Public Health Association, 2006). Although preterm birth rates in the United States have decreased slightly in recent years, these rates continue to be significantly higher than those in other developed countries, and disparities remain persistent and dramatic. For instance, premature births still occur 1.5 times more frequently in African American mothers compared with white mothers (March of Dimes Foundation [MODF], 2015). Efforts to decrease preterm birth rates continue, but prematurity remains a significant public health concern, as babies born prematurely experience both short-term and long-term adverse health outcomes. Even as progress is made in decreasing preterm birth rates, continued work is needed to identify effective strategies to reduce the negative consequences of premature birth, particularly among marginalized populations, which experience the largest disparities in negative infant health outcomes and possess fewer resources to manage challenges associated with prematurity.

One factor that has received little attention is the role of public policy in supporting or hindering parental involvement with babies who require hospitalization in neonatal intensive care units (NICUs) because of low birthweight (LBW), preterm birth, or both. Although evidence indicates that parental involvement through interventions such as kangaroo mother care (KMC), also known as "skin-to-skin care," leads to improvements in maternal and infant health and decreases in infant mortality, the United States remains the only developed country without universal paid parental leave. More research is needed to understand the degree to which parental involvement helps to decrease adverse outcomes from premature birth and to describe the role of supportive policies such as paid parental leave in facilitating parental involvement for those babies born early, with LBW, or both. Social workers, given their training, practice contexts, and mandate to advocate for marginalized populations, have the potential to make meaningful research contributions to reduce disparities and improve infant health outcomes.

PRETERM BIRTH AS BOTH A PUBLIC HEALTH AND A SOCIAL JUSTICE ISSUE

Infants born before 37 weeks gestation are identified as *premature* or *preterm* (MODF, 2014). Along with prematurity, the literature often references LBW as a key indicator of maternal and infant health. Infants born at LBW (that is, less than 5 lbs. 8 oz.) have often but not always been born prematurely (MODF, 2014). LBW infants are generally treated in the NICU along with many preterm infants. In the United States, one in eight infants is born prematurely. Although the rate of prematurity has declined slightly in recent years, it is still significantly higher than rates in previous decades (MODF, 2014). Among the reasons for this phenomenon are rising maternal age; advances in assisted reproductive technology leading to more multiple births, such as twins and triplets; and advanced medical technology facilitating the ability to keep premature and LBW babies alive when, in the past, they would likely have died (Cho et al., 2012). In addition to these factors, maternal stress is linked to rates of prematurity. Sources of stress include behavioral factors such as maternal diet and smoking (Cho et al., 2012) and social factors such as death of a family member during pregnancy (Witt et al., 2014). Chronic and cumulative stressors related to racism, poverty, and trauma may also cause maternal and child health disparities (Lu & Halfon, 2003; Mustilio et al., 2004), prompting many maternal and child health advocates to reorient services to better address these issues (Braveman, Egerter, & Mockenhaupt, 2011; Dominguez, 2010; Lu, 2014; Wilensky & Satcher, 2009).

Infants born prematurely potentially face numerous challenges to biopsychosocial well-being. Many infants born prematurely or with LBW need extensive medical care in NICUs and are at risk for subsequent medical complications, including intraventricular hemorrhage, bronchopulmonary dysplasia, respiratory distress, sepsis, and ultimately death (Schaaf, Mol, Abu-Hanna, & Ravelli, 2012). Assuming they survive and are discharged from NICU, children born prematurely have higher likelihoods of experiencing both physical and cognitive disabilities (Moster, Lie, & Markestad, 2008), as well as behavioral difficulties and autism spectrum disorder (Limperopoulos et al., 2008). In addition, premature infants often have difficulties in feeding, regulating emotions, meeting developmental milestones, and maintaining adequate immune system strength (Cho et al., 2012). The complex and unique needs of premature infants present mothers with extraordinary challenges that may influence maternal mental health, mother–infant bonding and attachment, child development, parenting stress, and social support (Cho et al., 2012). Finally, children surviving premature birth and LBW also often have academic and attention difficulties, impaired executive function, and delays compared with same-age peers; these difficulties frequently persist into adulthood (Aarnoudse-Moens, Weisglas-Kuperus, van Goudoever, & Oosterlaan, 2008).

Disparities in Preterm Births and Subsequent Health Outcomes

Whereas rates of prematurity are high across all populations in the United States, premature birth and adverse health outcomes are more likely to occur among those of low socioeconomic status (SES) and racial and ethnic minority populations. Women with low SES and women of color such as African Americans, American Indians, Alaskan Natives, and Latinas experience disproportionately high numbers of poor maternal and child health outcomes (American Public Health Association, 2011; Walker & Chesnut, 2010). Women with low SES are more likely to experience premature labor and birth, LBW babies (Blumenshine, Egerter, Barclay, Cubbin, & Braveman, 2010), and infant mortality (Braveman et al., 2011) compared with their more affluent counterparts. Furthermore, poverty levels are associated neonatal outcomes; that is, mothers experiencing greater levels of poverty have infants with worse neonatal outcomes (Olson, Diekema, Elliott, & Renier, 2010). In terms of racial and ethnic disparities, African American women, compared with white women, have twice the rate of LBW, are 60 percent more likely to have preterm births (Martin & Osterman, 2013), and have 2.3 times the rate of infant mortality (MacDorman & Mathews, 2013). Similarly, American Indians and Alaskan Natives have a 53 percent higher rate of infant mortality (MacDorman & Mathews, 2013) and higher rates of preterm birth compared with white infants (Martin & Osterman, 2013). Certain Latina groups also experience maternal and child health disparities, including a higher preterm birth rate (Martin & Osterman, 2013); for example, there is a 32 percent higher rate of infant mortality among Puerto Ricans (MacDorman & Mathews, 2013).

Costs of Prematurity and LBW

The consequences of preterm birth and LBW are challenging for children and their families, but they also come at an economic cost to society. In 2006, the Institute of Medicine estimated that the economic impact of preterm births in the United States was more than $26 billion (Behrman & Butler, 2007). Over $7 billion of this estimate was attributed to the costs of special education and loss of economic productivity because of the physical and cognitive disabilities experienced by those born prematurely. The estimate does not include lifetime medical costs associated with these conditions. These long-term economic consequences make the disparities in rates of prematurity of even greater concern: Not only are people of low SES and people of color more likely to experience premature birth, but their premature children are then more likely to experience lifelong social and economic disadvantages.

PARENTAL INVOLVEMENT AND INFANT HEALTH

The importance of parental involvement in the care of infants is well documented. Through interventions such as KMC, in which a mother has prolonged skin-to-skin contact with her baby, infants with consistent parental involvement demonstrate more stable body temperature, regulated sleep, improved neurological development, enhanced bonding (Kymre, 2014), increased breastfeeding, and reduced pain response (Nyqvist et al., 2010). Mothers who participate in KMC have lower rates of maternal depression and are more sensitive to recognizing infant behavior (Nyqvist et al., 2010). Some scholars hypothesize this sensitivity to infant behavior may be linked to rates of infant mortality—that mothers who are more attuned to their infants' behavior are more likely to respond to their needs and subsequently have lower rates of infant mortality (Rossin, 2011).

In addition to KMC, research points to the benefit of other forms of parental involvement. Integrating KMC with traditional clothed holding, family sessions, eye contact, emotional expression, and vocal soothing has been associated with better quality maternal caregiving behavior (Hane et al., 2015). Maternal visitation in the NICU and traditional blanket holding is linked to positive infant health indicators such as decreased arousal and improved physical movement (Reynolds et al., 2013).

Some researchers propose that interventions designed to promote maternal–infant bonding should be considered as strategies to decrease persistent disparities in neonatal health outcomes. In a longitudinal study of low-income, predominantly African American women, strategies promoting "maternal–fetal attachment" were found to be predictors of less LBW and fewer preterm births (Alhusen, Gross, Hayat, Woods, & Sharps, 2012). This study affirms the relationship between parental involvement and neonatal health, particularly among groups who historically experience poor maternal and infant health outcomes.

There is a significant gap in the literature on paternal involvement in the NICU and with premature infants. Although some studies have examined the effects of prematurity and NICU involvement on paternal mental health (Lefkowitz, Baxt, & Evans, 2010; Olshtain-Mann & Auslander, 2008), few studies have focused on how paternal involvement with premature infants affects infant health outcomes. In a randomized controlled trial, an intervention designed to increase both maternal and paternal empowerment and competence in parenting preterm infants demonstrated the ability to improve parental mental health, strengthen parent–child interactions, and decrease infants' hospital length of stay (Melnyk et al., 2006). More research is needed to understand the specific pathways by which parental involvement decreases the time infants spend in the hospital and to determine whether this involvement also improves long-term health outcomes for preterm infants.

PARENTAL INVOLVEMENT AS A SOCIAL POLICY ISSUE

In light of evidence that parental involvement improves health outcomes for both parents and infants, most developed countries—in fact, almost all countries around the globe—have instituted paid leave policies that allow parents to take leave from employment while receiving at least partial pay. Among Organisation for Economic Cooperation and Development (OECD) countries, the United States alone fails to offer any statutory paid leave for mothers; most countries offer paid leave to both mothers and fathers (OECD, 2015). Many countries have flexible leave policies that allow for extended leave in the case of unusual or unexpected events during pregnancy, such as illness of the mother or newborn. Thus, in most countries, mothers whose children are born early and require hospitalization are eligible for extended maternity leave. In 2013, only 26 percent of countries did not provide a statutory right to extended leave for illness or complications (International Labour Office [ILO], 2014). Extension of leave in the case of multiple births is less common, although 25 percent of countries do provide extensions of this type. It should be noted, however, that because incidence of preterm birth is higher with multiples, many mothers of multiples may qualify for extensions anyway. When offered, most leave extensions are paid (ILO, 2014).

The United States, through the Family and Medical Leave Act (FMLA) of 1993 (2012) (P.L. 103-3), mandates that employers with 50 or more employees provide 12 weeks of job-protected leave for workers to manage their own illnesses, care for a newborn or newly adopted child, or care for an immediate family member with an illness or disability. This leave, however, does not have to be paid and is not extended to all workers. As of 2012, only 60 percent of workers in the United States were eligible for FMLA leave (Abt Associates, 2014).

Despite the lack of federal legislation mandating paid maternity or parental leave, many employers and a few states or jurisdictions have adopted paid leave policies. For instance, California, Rhode Island, and New Jersey have established family leave insurance programs that provide up to six weeks of partially paid leave, which is structured as a public insurance program and financed through employee payroll deductions (Winston, 2014). In addition, many companies offer paid maternity or parental leave as a benefit. Even with these policies in place, however, only 11 percent of workers in private industry in the United States were eligible for some type of paid family leave in 2012 (Van Giezen, 2013). An additional 26 percent of employees have access to partial pay for family leave, although often this comes in the form of other types of accrued paid leave (for example, sick leave or vacation days) during the unpaid FMLA leave period (Abt Associates, 2014).

Unfortunately, there are disparities in access to paid parental leave, such that employees in high-wage and professional positions are far more likely to have access to this benefit. Only one-fifth of workers in low-wage jobs are eligible for paid maternity or family leave, and among workers who took leave in 2011, those with household incomes below the median were much more likely to have gone unpaid than were those with household incomes above the median (53 percent versus 18 percent; Abt Associates, 2014). Furthermore, 31 percent of workers who took unpaid leave cut short their time away from work because of financial concerns (Abt Associates, 2014). Although this measure is not limited to those taking maternity or parental leave, it does suggest that those who do not receive paid maternity leave may be more prone to shortening their leave. Nearly half of all workers who take FMLA leave report that they would take more leave if it were at least partially paid, and two-thirds report that it was somewhat difficult (32 percent) or very difficult (31 percent) to make ends meet while on leave (Abt Associates, 2014). It is important to note that over 9 percent of workers who reported an unmet need for leave gave newborn care as the reason time away from work was needed, and employees whose incomes were less than $35,000 per year and people of color were more than twice as likely to report an unmet need for leave. In other words, the populations experiencing disproportionately high negative infant health outcomes are the same populations reporting inadequate leave opportunities.

The disparity in access to paid leave may be directly related to disparities in maternal and child health, because those in low-wage jobs are less likely to have access to or to be able to afford unpaid maternity leave and are therefore less likely to experience the health advantages offered by high levels of parental involvement with infants. Research indicates that infants born to mothers with access to parental leave (that is, FMLA) have better birth and infant health outcomes than do those born to parents unable to access these benefits (Rossin, 2011). However, a research gap exists in examining the effects of parental leave on the health outcomes of infants requiring NICU care, specifically, and on whether access to paid leave leads to increases in parental involvement and, subsequently, better infant health outcomes. This area of inquiry is important, especially because disparities in access to paid leave coincide with disparities in frequency of preterm births and poor outcomes for preterm infants. Enabling low-income and minority parents to participate actively in care for preterm and LBW infants may lead to short- and long-term improvements in infant health, thereby reducing health disparities that occur across the life course.

SOCIAL WORK IMPLICATIONS

The reality that prematurity among marginalized populations represents perpetuated social, physical, and economic inequality presents a social justice issue that the social work profession is well poised to address. According to the National Association of Social Workers' (2008) *Code of Ethics*, social workers are called to advocate for marginalized populations, including women, children, ethnic or racial minorities, and people with low SES. Social workers are trained to assess and intervene in ecological contexts and to engage in interdisciplinary practice and research (Allen, 2012; Andrews, Darnell, McBride, & Gehlert, 2013). Moreover, social workers are effective research and practice partners with those in the public health and medical professions (Gehlert & Coleman, 2010). Thus, social workers are arguably among the best-equipped professionals to participate in research and practice that address prematurity and its associated challenges, particularly among marginalized groups.

For example, hospital social workers often work with families caring for infants in the NICU; in fact, many hospitals employ social workers to work specifically with NICUs (National Association of Perinatal Social Workers [NAPSW], 2014). These social workers screen for postpartum depression and other maternal mental health issues, provide resource education and referrals for families, facilitate parent support groups as well as individual and family counseling sessions, and assist with discharge planning. Social workers may also be involved in staff education and support to enhance other NICU professionals' understanding of the role of the social workers and to assist them in working with families that present particular challenges (NAPSW, 2014). Other relevant contexts of social work practice may include community health clinics, mental health clinics, private practices, public health agencies, developmental follow-up centers, family planning clinics, and adoption agencies, where social workers are likely to interact with families affected by the consequences of preterm birth (NAPSW, 2014).

In addition to social work practice with public health and medical professionals, advocacy is an important way in which social workers can have tremendous impact. In recent months, family leave policy has been in the media and political spotlight in the United States. Thus, the time may be right for legislative action at the federal or state level. This year, for instance, the White House sponsored a Summit on Working Families at which President Obama discussed the importance of paid family leave (Obama, 2014). Social workers and other maternal and child health advocates would be wise to capitalize on this momentum to improve infant health outcomes among some of the nation's most vulnerable populations.

CONCLUSION

The past decade has seen a dramatic increase in efforts to reduce disparities in rates of preterm birth and LBW, and, to some extent, these efforts are paying off. Nonetheless, rates of preterm birth in the United States remain high, and disparities persist in rates of preterm birth among racial and ethnic minorities and those with low SES. Prematurity and LBW are antecedents of a number of costly long-term disabilities and chronic illnesses and, as such, can be seen as important contributors to health disparities across the life course. Despite the attention given to this public health issue among researchers and the medical and public health communities, little empirical evidence exists about the role public policies have in facilitating or creating barriers to parental involvement in neonatal care and their subsequent impact on neonatal outcomes. More research is needed to understand whether adopting paid leave policies may facilitate improvements in outcomes for preterm infants and their mothers, thereby reducing health disparities across the life course. The time is right for the social work profession to make research and practice contributions in this area. **HSW**

REFERENCES

Aarnoudse-Moens, C. S., Weisglas-Kuperus, N., van Goudoever, J. B., & Oosterlaan, J. (2008). Meta-analysis of neurobehavioral outcomes in very preterm and/or very low birth weight children. *Pediatrics, 124*, 717–728. doi:10.1542/peds.2008-2816

Abt Associates. (2014). *Family and medical leave in 2012: Technical report*. Retrieved from http://www.dol.gov/asp/evaluation/fmla/FMLA-2012-Technical-Report.pdf

Alhusen, J. L., Gross, D., Hayat, M. J., Woods, A. B., & Sharps, P. W. (2012). The influence of maternal–fetal attachment and health practices on neonatal outcomes in low-income, urban women. *Research in Nursing & Health, 35*, 112–120. doi:10.1002/nur.21464

Allen, H. (2012). Is there a social worker in the house? Health care reform and the future of medical social work [Viewpoint]. *Health & Social Work, 37*, 183–186. doi:10.1093/hsw/hls021

American Public Health Association. (2006). *Reducing racial/ethnic and socioeconomic disparities in preterm and low birthweight births*. Retrieved from https://www.apha.org/policies-and-advocacy/public-health-policy-statements/policy-database/2014/07/18/10/01/reducing-racial-ethnic-and-socioeconomic-disparities-in-preterm-and-low-birthweight-births

American Public Health Association. (2011). *Reducing US maternal mortality as a human right*. Retrieved from https://www.apha.org/policies-and-advocacy/public-health-policy-statements/policy-database/2014/07/11/15/59/reducing-us-maternal-mortality-as-a-human-right

Andrews, C. M., Darnell, J. S., McBride, T. D., & Gehlert, S. (2013). Social work and implementation of the Affordable Care Act [Guest Editorial]. *Health & Social Work, 38*, 67–71.

Behrman, R. E., & Butler, A. S. (Eds.). (2007). *Preterm birth: Causes, consequences, and prevention*. Washington, DC: Institute of Medicine, Committee on Understanding Premature Birth and Assuring Healthy Outcomes.

Blumenshine, P., Egerter, S., Barclay, C. J., Cubbin, C., & Braveman, P. A. (2010). Socioeconomic disparities in adverse birth outcomes. *American Journal of Preventive Medicine, 39*, 263–272. doi:10.1016/j.amepre.2010.05.012

Braveman, P. A., Egerter, S. A., & Mockenhaupt, R. E. (2011). Broadening the focus: The need to address the social determinants of health. *American Journal of Preventive Medicine, 40*(Suppl. 1), S4–S18.

Cho, Y., Hirose, T., Tomita, N., Shirakawa, S., Murase, K., Komoto, K., et al. (2012). Infant mental health intervention for preterm infants in Japan: Promotions of maternal mental health, mother–infant interactions, and social support by providing continuous home visits until the corrected infant age of 12 months. *Infant Mental Health Journal, 34,* 47–59. doi:10.1002/imhj.21352

Dominguez, T. P. (2010). Adverse birth outcomes in African American women: The social context of persistent reproductive disadvantage. *Social Work in Public Health, 26,* 3–16.

Family and Medical Leave Act of 1993, P.L. 103-3, 29 U.S.C. §§ 2601–2654 (2012).

Gehlert, S., & Coleman, R. (2010). Using community-based participatory research to ameliorate cancer disparities. *Health & Social Work, 35,* 302–309.

Hane, A. A., Meyers, M. M., Hofer, M. A., Ludwig, R. J., Halperin, M. S., Austin, J., et al. (2015). Family nurture intervention improves quality of maternal caregiving in the neonatal intensive care unit: Evidence from a randomized controlled trial. *Journal of Developmental & Behavioral Pediatrics, 36,* 188–196.

International Labour Office. (2014). *Maternity and paternity at work: Law and practice across the world*. Retrieved from http://www.ilo.org/wcmsp5/groups/public/---dgreports/---dcomm/---publ/documents/publication/wcms_242615.pdf

Kymre, I. G. (2014). NICU nurses' ambivalent attitudes in skin-to-skin practice. *International Journal of Qualitative Studies on Health and Well-Being, 9,* Article 23297. doi:10.3402/qhw.v9.23297

Lefkowitz, D. S., Baxt, C., & Evans, J. R. (2010). Prevalence and correlates of posttraumatic stress and postpartum depression in parents of infants in the neonatal intensive care unit (NICU). *Journal of Clinical Psychology in Medical Settings, 17,* 230–237. doi:10.1007/s10880-010-9202-7

Limperopoulos, C., Bassan, H., Sullivan, N. R., Soul, J. S., Robertson, R. L., Moore, M., et al. (2008). Positive screening for autism in ex-preterm infants: Prevalence and risk factors. *Pediatrics, 121,* 758–765. doi:10.1542/peds.2007-2158

Lu, M. C. (2014). Improving maternal and child health outcomes across the life course: Where do we go from here? *Maternal and Child Health Journal, 18,* 339–343. doi:10.1007/s10995-013-1400-0

Lu, M. C., & Halfon, N. (2003). Racial and ethnic disparities in birth outcomes: A life-course perspective. *Maternal and Child Health Journal, 7,* 13–30.

MacDorman, M. F., & Mathews, T. J. (2013, November 22). Infant deaths—United States, 2005–2008. *Morbidity and Mortality Weekly Report, 62*(Suppl. 3), 171–175. Retrieved from http://www.cdc.gov/mmwr/preview/mmwrhtml/su6203a29.htm?s_cid=su6203a29_w

March of Dimes Foundation. (2014). *Low birthweight*. Retrieved from http://www.marchofdimes.com/baby/low-birthweight.aspx

March of Dimes Foundation. (2015). *March of Dimes 2015 premature birth report card*. Retrieved from http://www.marchofdimes.org/mission/prematurity-reportcard.aspx

Martin, J. A., & Osterman, M.J.K. (2013). Preterm births—United States, 2006 and 2010. *Morbidity and Mortality Weekly Report, 62*(Suppl. 3), 136–138. Retrieved from http://www.cdc.gov/mmwr/preview/mmwrhtml/su6203a22.htm?s_cid=su6203a22_w

Melnyk, B. M., Feinstein, N. F., Alpert-Gillis, L., Fairbanks, E., Crean, H. F., Sinkin, R. A., et al. (2006). Reducing premature infants' lengths of stay and improving parents' mental health outcomes with the Creating Opportunities for Parent Empowerment (COPE) Neonatal Intensive Care Unit Program: A randomized, controlled trial. *Pediatrics, 118,* e1414–e1427. doi:10.1542/peds.2005-2580

Moster, D., Lie, R. T., & Markestad, T. (2008). Long-term medical and social consequences of preterm birth. *New England Journal of Medicine, 359,* 262–273.

Mustilio, S., Krieger, N., Gunderson, E., Sidney, S., McCreath, H., & Kiefe, C. (2004). Self-reported experiences of racial discrimination and black–white differences in preterm and low-birthweight deliveries: The CARDIA Study. *American Journal of Public Health, 94,* 2125–2131.

National Association of Perinatal Social Workers. (2014). *About NAPSW*. Retrieved from http://www.napsw.org/about/about-napsw.html

National Association of Social Workers. (2008). *Code of ethics of the National Association of Social Workers*. Retrieved from http://www.socialworkers.org/pubs/code/code.asp

Nyqvist, K. H., Anderson, G. C., Bergman, N., Cattaneo, A., Charpak, N., Davanzo, R., et al. (2010). Towards universal kangaroo mother care: Recommendations and report from the First European Conference and Seventh International Workshop on Kangaroo Mother Care. *Acta Paediatrica, 99,* 820–826. doi:10.1111/j.1651-2227.2010.01787.x

Obama, B. (2014, June 23). *Remarks by President Obama at the White House Summit on Working Families* [Transcript]. Retrieved from http://www.whitehouse.gov/the-press-office/2014/06/23/remarks-president-obama-white-house-summit-working-families-june-23-2014

Olshtain-Mann, O., & Auslander, G. K. (2008). Parents of preterm infants two months after discharge from the hospital: Are they still at (parental) risk? *Health & Social Work, 33,* 299–308.

Olson, M. E., Diekema, D., Elliott, B. A., & Renier, C. M. (2010). Impact of income and income inequality on infant health outcomes in the United States. *Pediatrics, 126,* 1165–1173. doi:10.1542/peds.2009-3378

Organisation for Economic Cooperation and Development. (2015). *PF2.1: Key characteristics of parental leave systems*. Retrieved from http://www.oecd.org/els/soc/PF2_1_Parental_leave_systems.pdf

Reynolds, L. C., Duncan, M. M., Smith, G. C., Mathur, A., Neil, J., Inder, T., & Pineda, R. G. (2013). Parental presence and holding in the neonatal intensive care unit and associations with early neurobehavior. *Journal of Perinatology, 33,* 636–641. doi:10.1038/jp.2013.4

Rossin, M. (2011). The effects of maternity leave on children's birth and infant health outcomes in the United States. *Journal of Health Economics, 30,* 221–239. doi:10.1016/j.jhealeco.2011.01.005

Schaaf, J. M., Mol, B.-W. J., Abu-Hanna, A., & Ravelli, A.C.J. (2012). Ethnic disparities in the risk of adverse outcome after spontaneous preterm birth. *ACTA Obstetricia et Gynecologica Scandinavica, 91,* 1402–1408. doi:10.1111/aogs.12013

Van Giezen, R. W. (2013). Paid leave in private industry over the past 20 years. *Beyond the Numbers, 2*(18), 1–6.

Walker, L. O., & Chesnut, L. W. (2010). Identifying health disparities and social inequities affecting childbearing women and infants. *Journal of Obstetric, Gynecologic, & Neonatal Nursing, 39,* 328–338.

Wilensky, G. R., & Satcher, D. (2009). Don't forget about the social determinants of health. *Health Affairs, 28*(2), w194–w198.

Winston, P. (2014). *Work–family supports for low-income families: Key research findings and policy trends*. Retrieved from http://aspe.hhs.gov/hsp/14/WorkFamily/rpt_workfamily.cfm

Witt, W. P., Cheng, E. R., Wisk, L. E., Litzelman, K., Chatterjee, D., Mandell, K., & Wakeel, F. (2014).

Preterm birth in the United States: The impact of stressful life events prior to conception and maternal age. *American Journal of Public Health, 104*(Suppl. 1), S73–S80. doi:10.2105/AJPH.2013.301688

Jennifer C. Greenfield, PhD, *is assistant professor and* **Susanne Klawetter, LCSW,** *is a PhD candidate, Graduate School of Social Work, University of Denver. Address correspondence to Jennifer C. Greenfield, Graduate School of Social Work, University of Denver, 2148 S. High Street, Denver, CO 80208; e-mail: jennifer.greenfield@du.edu.*

Original manuscript received August 12, 2014
Accepted December 9, 2014
Advance Access Publication November 27, 2015

MACRO PERSPECTIVES ON YOUTHS AGING OUT OF FOSTER CARE

MARY E. COLLINS

For the past 20 years, there has been increased attention to the circumstances under which young adults leave the foster care system when they achieve age-defined adulthood. In the United States, this is referred to as "aging out" of foster care. Typically, young people did not benefit from a reunification with their family or a permanent family situation with kin or through adoption.

Macro Perspectives on Youths Aging Out of Foster Care offers an extensive look at this problem through a macro orientation. Attempting to balance the primary focus on microsystems, and consistent with a social work perspective, this book aims to provide a greater emphasis on the larger macrosystems of society, policy, organization, and community. Successful or unsuccessful outcomes of the transition from foster care are heavily dependent on the processes and structures that make up the external environment. Youths exiting foster care may be especially influenced by the circumstances of the larger social context because they often lack the mediating advantages of a strong familial connection. After long stays in the foster care system, they may have limited support, skills, and resources required for a healthy, productive, independent adulthood.

This reorientation of focus to macrosystems affecting the individual transition experience informs questions such as these: What are the barriers to developing and implementing effective approaches? How can we bring more social attention to these youths? How might communities better support youths? To what extent should policy and program supports be designed specifically for this population, as opposed to a more expansive population of vulnerable youths (such as youths receiving child welfare services in their homes, or youths involved in more than one service system), or more general universal supports for all youths?

Macro Perspectives on Youths Aging Out of Foster Care draws on research, theory, and practice to address these issues. It is a useful resource for practitioners in child welfare and youth services, researchers, and policymakers.

ISBN: 978-0-87101-488-7. 2015. Item #4887. 224 pages. $49.99

1-800-227-3590
www.naswpress.org

CODE:MPFC15

Female Genital Mutilation Is a Violation of Reproductive Rights of Women: Implications for Health Workers

Suresh Banayya Jungari

Female genital mutilation (FGM) comprises all procedures that involve partial or total removal of the external female genitalia or other injury to the female genital organs for nonmedical reasons. This coercive practice is still prevalent in many parts of the world, in both developed and developing countries. However, FGM is more prevalent in African countries and some Asian countries. In this study, an attempt has been made to understand the prevalence and practice of FGM worldwide and its adverse effects on women's reproductive health. To fulfill the study objectives, the author collected evidence from various studies conducted by international agencies. Many studies found that FGM has no health benefits; is mostly carried out on girls before they reach the age of 15 years; can cause severe bleeding, infections, psychological illness, and infertility; and, most important, can have serious consequences during childbirth. The practice is mainly governed by the traditions and cultures of the communities without having any scientific or medical benefit. In conclusion, FGM is a practice that violates the human and reproductive rights of women.

KEY WORDS: *community health work; excision; female genital mutilation; infertility; infibulations*

Female genital mutilation (FGM) comprises all procedures that involve partial or total removal of the external female genitalia or other injury to the female genital organs for nonmedical reasons. This practice is mostly carried out by traditional circumcisers, who often play other central roles in communities, such as attending childbirths. However, more than 18 percent of all FGM is performed by health care providers, and this trend is increasing (World Health Organization [WHO], 2013). FGM is also known by other names, like "female genital cutting" and "circumcision." The practice of FGM is deeply rooted in cultures and traditional customs. In this article, I explain the long-term reproductive consequences of FGM for women and how their reproductive rights are violated by communities around the world that practice this custom. WHO, Division of Family Health (1996), estimated that in 100 to 140 million girls and women had been subjected to one of several forms of genital mutilation, and more than 125 million women and girls live with FGM today (WHO, 2013). Most of these girls and women live in 28 African countries that widely accept this practice, although some live in the Middle East and Asia (see Table 1). This practice is also increasingly found among some immigrant population groups in Europe, the United States, Canada, Australia, and New Zealand (Dorkenoo, 2001).

FGM violates the human rights of girls when it is performed on them as infants or youths. The fundamental issue at stake here is that of child consent: A child, having no formed judgment, is unable to consent, but rather simply undergoes the mutilation while she is totally vulnerable (Dorkenoo, 1995; Plo, Asse, Seï, & Yenan, 2014). The causes for the continued practice of FGM represent a mix of cultural, religious, and social factors within families and communities. For instance, it is believed that FGM is important to maintain tradition and improve marriageability (Gibeau, 1998; Vissandjée, Kantiébo, Levine, & N'Dejuru, 2003; Yasin, Al-Tawil, Shabila, & Al-Hadithi, 2013). In certain tribes, a girl cannot be considered an adult unless she has undergone FGM.

FGM is an indicator of extreme gender discrimination among the communities practicing it. It is believed in these communities that, by performing this coercive act on children and women, they are preserving their cultural roots; many elderly women also strongly support it.

Table 1: Estimated Prevalence of Female Genital Mutilation (FGM) in Girls and Women (Ages 15–49) Worldwide

Country	Year	% Estimated Prevalence of FGM
Benin	2001	16.8
Burkina Faso	2005	72.5
Cameroon	2004	1.4
Central African Republic	2005	25.7
Chad	2004	44.9
Djibouti	2006	93.1
Eritrea	2002	88.6
Ethiopia	2005	74.2
Gambia	2005	78.3
Ghana	2005	3.8
Guinea	2005	95.6
Kenya	2003	32.2
Mali	2001	91.6
Nigeria	2003	19.0
Senegal	2005	28.2
Somalia	2005	97.9
Sudan	2000	90.0
Yemen	1997	22.6

Note: The estimates are derived from a variety of local and subnational studies (Yoder & Khan, 2007).

WHO classifies FGM into four major types (see Figure 1). The first, *clitoridectomy*, is the partial or total removal of the clitoris (a small, sensitive, and erectile part of the female genitals) or, in very rare cases, only the prepuce (the fold of skin surrounding the clitoris). The second, *excision*, is the partial or total removal of the clitoris and the labia minora, with or without excision of the labia majora (the labia are the lips that surround the vagina). The third, *infibulation*, is the narrowing of the vaginal opening through the creation of a covering seal. The seal is formed by cutting and repositioning the inner or outer labia, with or without removal of the clitoris. All other harmful procedures to the female genitalia for nonmedical purposes, for example, pricking, piercing, incising, scraping, and cauterizing the genital area, fall into the fourth category, *other*.

MEDICALIZATION OF FGM

The *medicalization of FGM* refers to situations in which FGM is practiced by health care providers in public or private clinics, at home, or in other medical settings. It also includes the procedure of reinfibulation (that is, the restitching or narrowing of the vaginal opening through the creation of a covering seal to close the vagina again after childbirth) at any point in a woman's life. Involvement of health care providers in this practice is another major issue of concern (United Nations Population Fund [UNFPA] et al., 2010) because health care providers well know the consequences of FGM practice. By conducting this practice, they create hurdles in eradicating FGM. However, many other experts in the field have different opinions on the practice of FGM. At the same time, the medicalization of FGM may contribute to the abandonment of this practice: When the negative health consequences inherent to this procedure become more apparent because more interventions to fix the negative consequences of FGM are needed, health care providers will help to understand the negative aspects of this practice. And some argue that having trained health care providers perform FGM can reduce the pain and maternal consequences of FGM and may be a sound and compassionate approach to improving women's health in settings where abandonment of the practice of FGM is not immediately attainable (Christoffersen-Deb, 2005; Shell-Duncan, 2001).

Health care providers who carry out FGM include physicians, assistant physicians, clinical officers, nurses, midwives, trained traditional birth attendants, and other personnel providing health care to the population in both the private and the public sectors (Njue & Askew, 2004). Some providers are officially retired but continue to provide FGM, as well as other health services. Medicalization gives the misleading impression that the procedure is good for health or that it is harmless. An unfortunate consequence of FGM medicalization is that some providers may develop a professional and financial interest in continuing the practice. Medicalization of FGM is also supported by elderly health care providers who want to uphold traditional values (Ugboma, Akani, & Babatunde, 2003).

OBJECTIVE

The objective of this review is to present the causes, prevalence, and health consequences of FGM and how women's and children's rights are being violated by this practice.

METHOD

To fulfill the study objectives, I collected evidence from various studies conducted by international agencies, published research papers, and reports of various nongovernmental organizations. Information from these sources was examined to ascertain

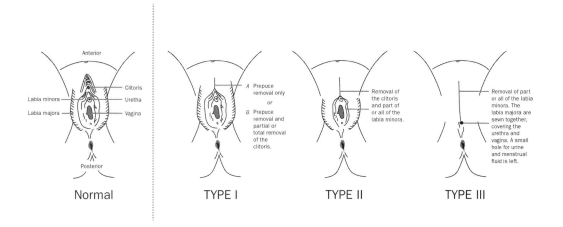

Figure 1: Types of Female Genital Mutilation

the current impact of FGM. Various international conventions have been reviewed to understand how such conventions can be used as instruments for the eradication of FGM. Various international conference proceedings have been extensively studied to explore expert and researcher opinions about these practices. Also, I emphasize the various international organizations' work related to the eradication of FGM.

Data about FGM are not available for all of the countries where FGM is prevalent, which hampers the full understanding of the current situation and the impact of FGM. Also, every country has its own specific demographic health survey, and these surveys are conducted in different time periods; therefore, it is difficult to establish the similarities between two or more countries over a specific time. Most of the studies are undertaken from medical or hospital-based perspectives; community-based studies and studies on psychological consequences of FGM are rare.

RESULTS AND DISCUSSION
FGM and Violation of Human Rights

FGM does not offer any health benefits for girls and women, but it does have several short-term as well as long-term consequences on girls' and women's health. This harmful, coercive practice directly violates the human rights of girls and women. FGM has been governed by social and religious beliefs rather than health concerns. The human rights perspective reveals deep-rooted inequality between the sexes; FGM, in this light, constitutes an extreme form of discrimination against women. Apart from this, extreme violations of children's rights are another issue of concern. FGM practices also violate one's rights to health, security, and physical integrity; the right to be free from torture and cruel, inhumane, or degrading treatment; and the right to life when the procedures result in death. FGM is recognized internationally as a violation of human rights because of its coercive nature, negative health consequences, and inherent risks.

FGM and Reproductive Health Outcomes

Many studies have shown the negative consequences of FGM on women's health in general and reproductive and sexual health in particular. The negative impact of FGM is more on maternal than neonatal outcomes during pregnancy and childbirth (Hakim, 2001; Jones, Diop, Askew, & Kabore, 1999). FGM is associated with urinary tract infections and adverse obstetric outcomes (Banks et al., 2006; De Silva, 1989; Kaplan, Hechavarría, Martín, & Bonhoure, 2011; Morison et al., 2001; Obermeyer, 2005). Women with FGM are significantly more likely than those without FGM to have adverse obstetric outcomes, and the risk is greater with more extensive FGM (Eke & Nkanginieme, 2006). Women who are subjected to FGM are also at greater risk of getting HIV infections. FGM has been supported by women who are unaware of the negative health aspects of the practice but are aware of the relative social value granted to the positive ones (Gallo, 1985). Elderly women's support for the practice is another issue of concern and has become a strong impediment to its elimination. The lack of awareness and knowledge about its serious consequences for women is another factor for FGM's support within the community (Yasin et al., 2013). Support from families and elderly women for FGM practice is strong in communities where FGM is more prevalent.

FGM and Sexual Health Outcomes

The practice of FGM is intended to prevent female sexual desire, thereby protecting a girl's virginity for her future husband. Control over girls' or women's sexuality through FGM is accepted in African communities in which the practice is high. When FGM is performed on a girl or woman, full enjoyment of her rights and liberties are, in effect, taken away from her (United Nations Children's Fund, 2005). Sexual function is adversely affected by FGM: Sexual quality of life is significantly lower for those women who have undergone FGM compared with those who have not (Alsibiani & Rouzi, 2010; Andersson, Rymer, Joyce, Momoh, & Gayle, 2012). For example, women who have undergone FGM have difficulty achieving orgasm by direct stimulation of the external clitoris. Surgical defibulation releases the infibulation scar and appears to improve sexual functioning but not orgasm (Paterson, Davis, & Binik, 2012).

FGM and Physical Health Outcomes

Bleeding. FGM damages arteries and veins. Primary hemorrhaging during the operation is unavoidable (secondary hemorrhaging may appear later if, for example, the wound becomes infected). Serious bleeding can lead to shock and even death.

Shock. Shock may arise not only from bleeding, but also from pain and fear. It can prove fatal.

Infection and Septicaemia. In less than optimal conditions, such as when FGM is performed in closed, poorly lit spaces with instruments that have not been sterilized, infection is a likely outcome of any operation. The practice of binding a patient's legs after FGM aggravates any infection by preventing drainage from the wound. Infection may spread inward, penetrating the vagina and passing into the uterus and ovaries, causing chronic pelvic infection and infertility. Development of tetanus may cost the patient her life. Septicaemia, also potentially fatal, is a possible complication from serious infection.

Urine Retention. After FGM, urination may be difficult or impossible. The urinary canal may be partially or entirely obstructed. Pain or fear of pain during urination may prevent natural flow. *Edema* (the presence of an excessive amount of fluid in or around cells, tissues, or serous cavities of the body) or other wound reactions (for example, granulation tissue or fibrosis) may contribute to obstruction.

Menstrual Problems. Normal menstruation may be hindered by partial or total occlusion of the vaginal opening. This may result in *dysmenorrhea* (painful menstrual periods); painful menstruation; or, in acute cases, *hematocolpos*, the accumulation of menstrual blood in the vagina and uterus. Distension of the abdomen induced by the accumulation of menstrual blood, together with the lack of any outward evidence of menstruation, may prompt suspicion of pregnancy. In a society where men guard the honor of their families, should suspicions of extramarital relations arise, the unfortunate woman may be put to death.

Difficult Micturition. Obstruction of the urinary opening or damage to the urinary canal may, in time, cause several complications, including painful urination. Urinary tract infections can lead to a similar state.

Urinary Tract Infection. Infibulations create a bridge of skin that obscures the opening of the urinary canal. The normal flow of urine is deflected, and the area remains constantly wet and susceptible to bacterial infection. Such infection may spread throughout the urinary tract, affecting both the bladder and the kidneys.

Calculus Formation. Menstrual debris or urinary deposits in the vagina or behind the bridge of skin created during FGM may calcify, forming a kind of stone or stones. *Calculus*, or stone formation, is also possible, encapsulating foreign matter in the vagina. Calculus formation may cause fistulae.

Fistulae and Incontinence. A *fistula* is a canal or connection between the urinary tract and vagina (vesicovaginal) or between the rectum and vagina (rectovaginal), which causes incontinence.

FGM and Psychological Outcomes

FGM has a number of negative psychological outcomes that are extremely harmful for girls and women. For example, FGM could lead to depression, anxiety, and neuroses (Baasher, 1979; Khalaf, 2013; Rushwan, 2013). Feelings of incompleteness, fear, inferiority, and suppression among women who have undergone FGM are higher compared with women who have not undergone FGM. They are also at higher risk of psychiatric and psychosomatic diseases, which are characterized by physical symptoms resulting from psychological factors, usually involving a system of the body such as the gastrointestinal or genitourinary system (Utz-Billing & Kentenich, 2008). Comparative clinical studies found that circumcised women, compared with uncircumcised women, showed a significantly higher prevalence of posttraumatic stress disorder (PTSD) and other psychiatric disorders. PTSD was accompanied by memory problems (Behrendt & Moritz, 2005; Elnashar & Abdelhady, 2007), feelings of loss of trust, a prevailing lack of bodily well-being, posttraumatic shock, and depression among women and girls who had undergone an FGM procedure (Lax, 2000). Physical health outcomes also contribute to increases in psychological stress. More research is needed to fully understand the psychological outcomes of FGM.

INTERNATIONAL INSTRUMENTS FOR ERADICATION OF FGM

The Universal Declaration of Human Rights (United Nations, 1948) proclaimed the right of all human beings to live in conditions that enable them to enjoy good health and health care (art. 25). This convention provides enough rights to every individual to prevent the FGM practice. The International Covenant on Economic, Social and Cultural Rights (United Nations, 1966) condemned discrimination on the grounds of gender and recognizes the universal right to the highest attainable standard of physical and mental health (art. 12). The Convention on the Elimination of All Forms of Discrimination against Women (United Nations, 1979) is another instrument that can be used to support the abandonment of FGM. Among its mandates are to take all appropriate measures to modify or abolish customs and practices that constitute discrimination against women (art. 2f) and to modify social and cultural patterns of conduct of men and women. The goal of this convention is to eliminate prejudices, customs, and all practices that are based on beliefs about the inferiority or the superiority of either of the sexes (art. 5a). The Convention on the Rights of the Child (United Nations, 1989) protects against all forms of mental and physical violence and maltreatment (art. 19.1); emphasizes the need for freedom from torture or cruel, inhumane, or degrading treatment (art. 37a); and requires states to take all effective and appropriate measures to abolish traditional practices prejudicial to the health of children (art. 24.3).

The Programme of Action of the International Conference on Population and Development (United Nations, 1994) calls for governments to promote human rights of women and girls so that they can experience freedom from coercion, discrimination, violence, harmful practices, and sexual exploitation and to review national legislation and amend laws that discriminate against women and girls. It also calls for governments to ensure their health providers are knowledgeable and trained to serve clients who have been subjected to harmful practices. The report of Fourth World Conference on Women, in Beijing (United Nations, 1996), includes a section on girls and urges governments, international organizations, and nongovernmental organizations to develop policies and programs to eliminate all forms of discrimination against girls, including FGM.

Above all, conventions can be used as instruments for the elimination of the coercive practice of FGM. In fact, each and every convention named here promotes the dismissal of cultural practices that are harmful or discriminate against women on the basis of gender.

INTERNATIONAL EFFORTS FOR THE ELIMINATION OF FGM

Many international agencies are working to eliminate FGM. WHO is particularly concerned about the elimination of the practice (WHO, United Nations Children's Fund [UNICEF], UNFPA, 1997). The WHO, UNICEF, and UNFPA issued a new statement that built on the original from 1997. Great efforts have been made to counteract FGM, through research, work within communities, and changes in public policy believed to encourage progress at both international and local levels, where ingrained cultural beliefs need to be combated.

In 2008, WHO and nine other United Nations partners issued a new statement on the elimination of FGM to support increased advocacy for the abandonment of FGM. In 2010, WHO, in collaboration with other key United Nations agencies, published a global strategy to stop health care provider involvement in FGM (UNFPA et al., 2010). Furthermore, in 2012, the United Nations General Assembly accepted a resolution on the elimination of FGM.

ROLE OF THE SOCIAL WORKER

The practice of FGM is deeply embedded in cultures and communities. Therefore, local and international social workers play an imperative role in eradicating the practice and reducing the consequences, both physical and psychological, of FGM. They can do this by

- understanding the community beliefs about FGM and creating awareness about the negative health consequences of FGM
- educating older generations about negative health outcomes, particularly reproductive health outcomes
- conducting community-level awareness programs, in which individual and family meetings with local health workers or social workers are used to motivate and empower the community not to perform FGM on their children
- launching a large-scale campaign with local community heads and various community leaders
- counseling the girls on whom FGM has been performed to overcome the resulting psychological fear and help them to develop coping skills to deal with future consequences of FGM.

CONCLUSION

The practice of FGM has serious short-term and long-term consequences for girls and women, and these effects are especially harmful during pregnancy and childbirth. It is also evident that FGM practice is governed by cultural and traditional customs. To eradicate FGM, strong efforts at international and community levels are needed. Creating awareness among the communities about negative outcomes of the practice is essential to accelerating its abandonment. But protecting women and girls against harmful practices remains a challenge. The results of an ongoing International Conference on Population and Development Beyond 2014 (2014) global review reveal that only 46.2 percent of countries have promulgated and enforced laws protecting girls against harmful practices, including FGM; this percentage is as high as 66 percent in Africa. Discrimination against women and girls, including harmful traditional practices, is a violation of women's fundamental human rights and remains the most pervasive and persistent form of gender inequality.

Because FGM is a manifestation of gender inequality, the empowerment of women, especially economic empowerment, is key to its eradication. Gainful employment gives women confidence and influence in various spheres of their lives, influencing sexual and reproductive health choices, education, and healthy behavior (UNFPA, 2007). To that end, health and social workers can play critical roles in eradicating FGM. **HSW**

REFERENCES

Alsibiani, S. A., & Rouzi, A. A. (2010). Sexual function in women with female genital mutilation. *Fertility and Sterility, 93*, 722–724.

Andersson, S.H.A., Rymer, J., Joyce, D. W., Momoh, C., & Gayle, C. M. (2012). Sexual quality of life in women who have undergone female genital mutilation: A case–control study. *BJOG: An International Journal of Obstetrics & Gynaecology, 119*, 1606–1611.

Baasher, T. (1979, February 10–15). Psychological aspects of female circumcision. In WHO/EMRO Technical Publication 2, *Traditional practices affecting the health of women and children* (pp. 71–105). Geneva: World Health Organization.

Banks, E., Meirik, O., Farley, T., Akande, O., Bathija, H., & Ali, M. (2006). Female genital mutilation and obstetric outcome: WHO collaborative prospective study in six African countries. *Lancet, 367*, 1835–1841.

Behrendt, A., & Moritz, S. (2005). Posttraumatic stress disorder and memory problems after female genital mutilation. *American Journal of Psychiatry, 162*, 1000–1002.

Christoffersen-Deb, A. (2005). Taming tradition: Medicalized female genital practices in western Kenya. *Medical Anthropology Quarterly, 19*, 402–418.

De Silva, S. (1989). Obstetric squeal of female circumcision. *European Journal of Obstetric and Gynecological Reproductive Biology, 32*, 233–240.

Dorkenoo, E. (1995). *Cutting the rose: Female genital mutilation. The practice and its prevention*. London: Minority Rights Publications.

Dorkenoo, E. (2001, August). *Female genital mutilation: Human rights and cultural relativity*. Paper presented at Culture and Human Rights, Challenges and Opportunities for Human Rights Work workshop, Siem Reap, Cambodia.

Eke, N., & Nkanginieme, K.E.O. (2006). Female genital mutilation and obstetric outcome. *Lancet, 367*, 1799–1800. doi:10.1016/S0140-6736(06)68782-5

Elnashar, A., & Abdelhady, R. (2007). The impact of female genital cutting on health of newly married women. *International Journal of Gynecology & Obstetrics, 97*, 238–244.

Gallo, P. G. (1985). Female circumcision in Somalia: Some psychosocial aspects. *Genus, 41*(1–2), 133–147.

Gibeau, A. M. (1998). Female genital mutilation: When a cultural practice generates clinical and ethical dilemmas. *Journal of Obstetric, Gynecologic & Neonatal Nursing, 27*, 85–91.

Hakim, L. Y. (2001). Impact of female genital mutilation on maternal and neonatal outcomes during parturition. *East African Medical Journal, 78*, 255–258.

International Conference on Population and Development Beyond 2014. (2014). *Framework of actions for the follow-up to the programme of action of the ICPD beyond 2014*. Retrieved from http://icpdbeyond2014.org/about/view/29-global-review-report#sthash.qGByS4fg.dpuf

Jones, H., Diop, N., Askew, I., & Kabore, I. (1999). Female genital cutting practices in Burkina Faso and Mali and their negative health outcomes. *Studies in Family Planning, 30*, 219–230.

Kaplan, A., Hechavarría, S., Martín, M., & Bonhoure, I. (2011). Health consequences of female genital mutilation/cutting in the Gambia, evidence into action. *Reproductive Health, 8*, Article 26.

Khalaf, I. (2013). Editorial: Female genital cutting/mutilation in Africa deserves special concern: An overview. *African Journal of Urology, 19*, 119–122.

Lax, R. F. (2000). Socially sanctioned violence against women: Female genital mutilation is its most brutal form. *Clinical Social Work Journal, 28*, 403–412.

Morison, L., Scherf, C., Ekpo, G., Paine, K., West, B., Coleman, R., & Walraven, G. (2001). The long-term reproductive health consequences of female genital cutting in rural Gambia: A community-based survey. *Tropical Medicine & International Health, 6*, 643–653.

Njue, C., & Askew, I. (2004). *Medicalization of female genital cutting among the Abagusii in Nyanza Province, Kenya* (Frontiers in Reproductive Health Program Population Council report). Retrieved from http://pdf.usaid.gov/pdf_docs/Pnadb241.pdf

Obermeyer, C. M. (2005). The consequences of female circumcision for health and sexuality: An update on the evidence. *Culture, Health & Sexuality: An International Journal for Research, Intervention and Care, 7*, 443–461.

Paterson, L.Q.P., Davis, S. N., & Binik, Y. M. (2012). Female genital mutilation/cutting and orgasm before and after surgical repair. *Sexologies, 21*, 3–8.

Plo, K., Asse, K., Seï, D., & Yenan, J. (2014). Female genital mutilation in infants and young girls: Report of sixty cases observed at the General Hospital of Abobo (Abidjan, Cote D'Ivoire, West Africa). *International Journal of Pediatrics, 2014*, Article 837471.

Rushwan, H. (2013). Female genital mutilation: A tragedy for women's reproductive health. *African Journal of Urology, 19*, 130–133.

Shell-Duncan, B. (2001). The medicalization of female "circumcision": Harm reduction or promotion of a dangerous practice? *Social Sciences and Medicine, 52*, 1013–1028.

Ugboma, H. A., Akani, C. I., & Babatunde, S. (2003). Prevalence and medicalization of female genital mutilation. *Nigerian Journal of Medicine: Journal of the National Association of Resident Doctors of Nigeria, 13*, 250–253.

United Nations. (1948). *Universal Declaration of Human Rights* (General Assembly Resolution 217A [III], United Nations Doc. A/810 at 71). Retrieved from http://www.un.org/en/universal-declaration-human-rights/

United Nations. (1966). *International Covenant on Economic, Social and Cultural Rights* (General Assembly Resolution 2200A [XXI], 21 United Nations GAOR Supp. [No. 16] at 49, United Nations Doc. A/6316 [1966], 993 U.N.T.S. 3), entered into force January 3, 1976.

United Nations. (1979). *Convention on the Elimination of All Forms of Discrimination against Women* (1249 U.N.T.S. 13). Retrieved from http://www.un.org/womenwatch/daw/cedaw/text/econvention.htm

United Nations. (1989). *Convention on the Rights of the Child* (General Assembly Resolution 44/25, annex, 44 United Nations GAOR Supp. [No. 49] at 167, United Nations Doc. A/44/49 [1989]), entered into force September 2, 1990.

United Nations. (1994). *Report of the International Conference on Population and Development* (UN document A/Conf.171/13). Retrieved from http://www.un.org/popin/icpd/conference/offeng/poa.html

United Nations. (1996). *Report of the Fourth World Conference on Women, Beijing, 4–15 September 1995* (A/CONF/177/20). New York: Author.

United Nations Children's Fund. (2005). *Female genital mutilation/cutting: A statistical exploration*. New York: Author.

United Nations General Assembly. (2012, December 20). *Intensifying global efforts for the elimination of female genital mutilations* (Resolution 67/146). Geneva: Author.

United Nations Population Fund. (2007). *Women's economic empowerment: Meeting the needs of impoverished women*. New York: Author.

United Nations Population Fund, United Nations Human Rights Council, United Nations Children's Fund, United Nations Development Fund for Women, World Health Organization, International Federation of Gynaecology and Obstetrics, et al. (2010). *Global strategy to stop health-care providers from performing female genital mutilation* (WHO/RHR/10.9). Retrieved from http://www.who.int/reproductivehealth/publications/fgm/rhr_10_9/en/

Utz-Billing, I., & Kentenich, H. (2008). Female genital mutilation: An injury, physical and mental harm. *Journal of Psychosomatic Obstetrics & Gynecology, 29*, 225–229.

Vissandjée, B., Kantiébo, M., Levine, A., & N'Dejuru, R. (2003). The cultural context of gender, identity: Female genital, excision and infibulation. *Health Care for Women International, 24*, 115–124.

World Health Organization. (2008). *Eliminating female genital mutilation: An interagency statement—OHCHR, UNAIDS, UNDP, UNECA, UNESCO, UNFPA, UNHCR, UNICEF, UNIFEM, WHO*. Geneva: Author.

World Health Organization. (2013). *Female genital mutilation* (Fact Sheet No. 241). Retrieved from http://www.who.int/mediacentre/factsheets/fs241/en/

World Health Organization, Division of Family Health. (1996). *Female genital mutilation: Report of a WHO Technical Working Group, Geneva, 17–19 July 1995* (WHO/FRH/WHD/96.10). Geneva: Author.

World Health Organization, United Nations Children's Fund, United Nations Population Fund. (1997). *Female genital mutilation: A joint WHO/UNICEF/UNFPA statement*. Geneva: World Health Organization.

Yasin, B. A., Al-Tawil, N. G., Shabila, N. P., & Al-Hadithi, T. S. (2013). Female genital mutilation among Iraqi Kurdish women: A cross-sectional study from Erbil city. *BMC Public Health, 13*, Article 809.

Yoder, P. S., & Khan, S. (2007). *Numbers of women circumcised in Africa: The production of a total*. Calverton, MD: Macro International Inc.

Suresh Banayya Jungari, PhD, *is a scholar, International Institute for Population Sciences, Govandi Station Road, Deonar, Mumbai, Maharashtra 400088, India; e-mail: sureshjungariiips@gmail.com.*

Original manuscript received February 24, 2014
Final revision received October 4, 2014
Accepted December 9, 2014
Advance Access Publication December 27, 2015

HARM REDUCTION

for High-Risk Adolescent Substance Abusers

Maurice S. Fisher Sr.

In today's society, adolescents are faced with several life-changing challenges—peer pressure, bullying, alcohol and drug abuse, diseases, and engaging in various sexual behaviors.

In *Harm Reduction for High-Risk Adolescent Substance Abusers*, Maurice S. Fisher Sr. shares his experience of helping adolescent clients take charge of their life after negative consequences of substance use or abuse, and empowering young men and women to make better choices and minimize risky behaviors, using harm reductive methods.

Harm Reduction for High-Risk Adolescent Substance Abusers provides the research, discussion, and specific clinical techniques that can be used in private practices. Cognitive–behavioral therapy and skill development, psychoeducational and interpersonal skills, anger management, and support group therapies are discussed, as are ethical issues that may come up in practice.

The book serves as a good resource for therapists, counselors, and clinicians to help adolescents who have lost control and are signaling for help to get their life back on track and grow into adulthood as successful members of society.

ISBN: 978-0-87101-455-9   2014   Item #4559
230 pages $44.99
1-800-227-3590   www.naswpress.org

CODE: APHR14

Impact of Death Work on Self: Existential and Emotional Challenges and Coping of Palliative Care Professionals

Wallace Chi Ho Chan, Agnes Fong, Karen Lok Yi Wong, Doris Man Wah Tse, Kam Shing Lau, and Lai Ngor Chan

---

Palliative care professionals, such as social workers, often work with death and bereavement. They need to cope with the challenges on "self" in working with death, such as coping with their own emotions and existential queries. In this study, the authors explore the impact of death work on the self of palliative care professionals and how they perceive and cope with the challenges of self in death work by conducting a qualitative study. Participants were recruited from the palliative care units of hospitals in Hong Kong. In-depth interviews were conducted with 22 palliative care professionals: five physicians, 11 nurses, and six social workers. Interviews were transcribed to text for analysis. Emotional challenges (for example, aroused emotional distress from work) and existential challenges (for example, shattered basic assumptions on life and death) were identified as key themes. Similarly, emotional coping (for example, accepting and managing personal emotions) and existential coping (for example, rebuilding and actualizing life-and-death assumptions) strategies were identified. This study enhances the understanding of how palliative care professionals perceive and cope with the challenges of death work on the self. Findings may provide insights into how training can be conducted to enhance professionals' self-competence in facing these challenges.

KEY WORDS: *competence; coping; death; palliative care; self*

Palliative care has been continuously advancing worldwide (Lynch, Connor, & Clark, 2013). In different cultural contexts, social workers often work with different helping professionals in multidisciplinary teams providing palliative care (Brandsen, 2005; W.C.H. Chan, 2013). In fact, successful palliative care largely depends on the joint efforts of palliative care professionals, such as physicians, nurses, and social workers. Although these professionals play different roles in palliative care, they are all confronted by death in their work. They often work with dying patients and bereaved families, which may cause them great stress (Melvin, 2012; Slocum-Gori, Hemsworth, Chan, Carson, & Kazanjian, 2013). Research indicates that death and dying are sources of occupational stress in palliative care (Payne, 2001; Slocum-Gori et al., 2013). Palliative care professionals may experience various emotional and existential challenges in work, for example, arousal of strong emotional reactions and awareness of their own mortality (Zambrano, Chur-Hansen, & Crawford, 2014). Death and dying have a great impact on the personal lives and practice of palliative care professionals (Sinclair, 2011). These challenges emerging from working with death may affect not only their well-being but also their quality of care (Sanchez-Reilly et al., 2013).

However, a systematic review of previous studies showed that palliative care professionals do not necessarily experience a level of burnout higher than that experienced by health care professionals working in other contexts (Pereira, Fonseca, & Carvalho, 2011). The key seems to be whether they are competent in coping with the stress and challenges of palliative care (Desbiens & Fillion, 2007; Peters et al., 2012; Sanchez-Reilly et al., 2013). The ability to cope with the challenges of working in palliative care, where death is often encountered, is a competence that palliative care professionals have to acquire.

Gamino and Ritter (2012) proposed the term *death competence* to "describe specialized skill in tolerating and managing a client's problems related to dying, death, and bereavement" (p. 23). This competence highlights the importance of the ability of helping professionals to manage the impact of death on their self, such as their own death-related feelings. Previous discussions on what competencies should be cultivated in palliative care training and education focus on knowledge and skills for helping patients and their families (Bosma et al., 2010; Frey, Gott, Banfield, & Campbell, 2011; Meo, Hwang, & Morrison, 2011; Steven, White, & Marples, 2014), but relatively few focus on how helping professionals may develop the specific competence that helps them cope with the challenges of the work on their personal self. W.C.H. Chan and Tin (2012) referred to this kind of competence as *self-competence* in death work, which includes helping professionals' possession of essential personal resources (for example, optimism) and their ability to cope with emotions and existential issues aroused by death work (emotional coping and existential coping). *Death work* is defined as "any supportive, therapeutic or remedial work in response to death or matters related to death" (W.C.H. Chan & Tin, 2012, p. 900). Previous studies also suggest that it is crucial for palliative care professionals to find ways of coping with the emotions aroused by their work, for example, handling their own grief following the death of patients (Keene, Hutton, Hall, & Rushton, 2010) and developing emotional intelligence to help in facing the suffering of patients and bereaved families (Bailey, Murphy, & Porock, 2011). They may also need to cope with various existential challenges in their work, for example, addressing concerns such as spirituality (Clark et al., 2007), meaning in life (Sinclair, 2011), death attitudes, and values on death-related issues (Gwyther et al., 2005; Prochnau, Liu, & Boman, 2003).

To further understand the self-competence of palliative care professionals in facing death, dying, and bereavement, we aimed in this study to explore the impact of death work on the self of these professionals and how they perceive and cope with the challenges of self in death work. "Self" is a term often used in social work (Chinnery & Beddoe, 2011; Edwards & Bess, 1998). *Self* may be defined as helping professionals' personality traits, beliefs systems, and life experience (Dewane, 2006, p. 544). In this study, with reference to our earlier work on self-competence (W.C.H. Chan & Tin, 2012), we define *self* broadly as helping professionals' emotions, thoughts, beliefs, and behaviors.

METHOD
Research Design
Thematic analysis was used to underpin this study (Braun & Clarke, 2006). We used this qualitative approach to identify the key themes that may illustrate how palliative care professionals perceive and cope with the challenges of death work on self. We sought ethical approval from the research ethics committees of participating hospitals in this study. The consolidated criteria for reporting qualitative research guidelines (better known as the COREQ guidelines) were applied (Tong, Sainsbury, & Craig, 2007).

Interviewers
A research assistant with a master's degree conducted the interviews. She was trained by Wallace Chi Ho Chan and Agnes Fong (both are experienced social workers and thanatologists) before the interviews and conducted the first three interviews with their on-site guidance.

Participants
Participants, who were physicians, nurses, and social workers who had worked in palliative care for at least six months, were purposively recruited from three palliative care units of public hospitals in Hong Kong. Doris Man Wah Tse, Kam Shing Lau, and Lai Ngor Chan were the senior physicians or nurses working in these units. They helped to identify appropriate colleagues to join this study. Participants with different profiles were recruited to obtain variety in age, gender, and working experience specifically in palliative care. Written consent was obtained from all participants.

Data Collection
In-depth interviews were conducted with each participant in a semistructured format in their workplace. Two pilot interviews were conducted by Wallace Chi Ho Chan, Agnes Fong, and a research assistant. The initial interview guidelines were modified after the pilot interviews. Participants were invited to describe their daily work and illustrate how it might be different from their previous duties in other units, which was a conversation that might open a discussion on the effect of death work on the self. Follow-up questions were then asked, for example, "Apart from knowledge and skills, what are the challenges in your work? Do these challenges have any impact on you personally?" Participants were invited to give examples to illustrate what these challenges are, how they were influenced by these challenges, and how they coped with them. Each interview lasted from 60 to 90 minutes.

Analysis

All interviews were audio recorded, then transcribed to text for analysis. Field notes were also recorded during the interviews. The transcripts were sent to participants and verified by them. All participants acknowledged that the transcripts accurately reflected what they had shared.

To enhance the credibility of the findings, we used methods triangulation and analyst triangulation (Patton, 1999, p. 1193). Two levels of data analysis, with different methods of data analysis and different analysts, were conducted. At the first level, the research assistant analyzed the qualitative data using NVivo (Version 9) (Richards, 2015). She did the open coding by reading the transcripts line by line. Initial codes were given to different segments of text before major themes were identified. At the second level, Wallace Chi Ho Chan and Agnes Fong analyzed the data again with reference to the framework of W.C.H. Chan and Tin (2012). Coding was then conducted independently, and themes were identified. Themes identified at the first and second levels were compared. All themes identified at the first level were compatible with those at the second level; that is, most themes identified at these two levels were similar in meaning and could be reconceptualized into common themes, and differences could be resolved by reconceptualization into broader themes. After thorough comparison between the analyses at levels 1 and 2, themes were finalized.

RESULTS

Twenty-two palliative care professionals participated in this study: five physicians, 11 nurses, and six social workers. The majority of them were women (17 participants). Details are shown in Table 1.

Two key themes, challenges and coping, which interact with each other, were identified. Participants reported the *challenges* as situations in which they felt affected personally by death in their work, and they referred to *coping* as how they tried to cope with these challenges. Under the main theme of challenges, existential challenges and emotional challenges were identified as subthemes. Similarly, under the main theme of coping, existential coping and emotional coping were identified. The term "existential" was used to describe how participants perceived the challenges and adopted the coping in relation to their queries on existence, including assumptions on life and death and meaning in life and suffering. The term "emotional" was used to describe

Table 1: Background Information of Participants

Characteristic	N	%
Gender		
Men	5	23
Women	17	77
Religion		
Protestant	13	59
Catholic	3	14
Not religious	5	23
Buddhist	1	5
Years of experience in profession		
5 or less	4	18
6–10	3	14
11–15	5	23
16–20	7	32
21–25	1	5
26 or more	2	9
Years of experience in palliative care		
5 or less	10	45
6–10	8	36
11–15	3	14
16–20	1	5

the challenges that aroused their emotions (for example, helplessness and grief) and the coping that was used to manage these emotions. Figure 1 shows all of the key themes and subthemes identified in this study. All of the subthemes under the two main themes, challenges and coping, were identified and reported as follows.

Existential Challenges: Shattered Basic Life and Death Assumptions

Participants perceived the shattering of basic life and death assumptions to be the main existential challenge in death work. For example, they found it hard to see a young patient die, because this violates their assumption that elderly people should die first. Participants also found it difficult to understand why bad things happen to good people when they witnessed a kindhearted patient experience great pain and suffering. Findings revealed that the shattering included three subtle processes: awareness or confrontation of the nature of life and death, discrepancy from old self-beliefs, and reactions of distress and confusion. For example, one participant shared the observation, "I sometimes feel sorry for my patients why they are unable to achieve a life without regret despite trying very hard.... This makes me feel upset" (Participant 6). Another participant stated, "I was unhappy. This was related to my patient. I was

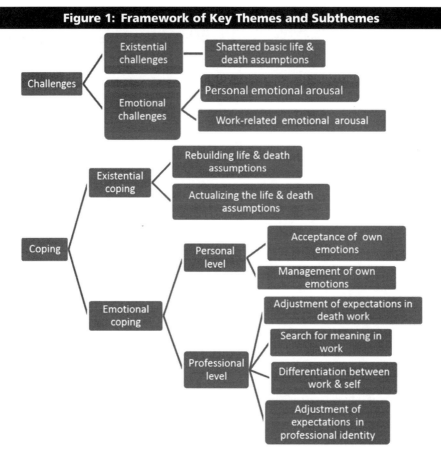

Figure 1: Framework of Key Themes and Subthemes

angry. . . . Why did a hardworking family man receive such punishment?" (Participant 22).

Emotional Challenges: Emotional Distress Related to Personal Life and Professional Work

Two types of emotional challenge, personal emotional arousal and work-related emotional arousal, were identified. Personal emotions were aroused when death work forced the participants to confront death-related concerns in their personal lives, such as participants' own death anxiety, past grief, regrets, and unfinished business. For example, one participant shared her worries of enduring cancer: "Thoughts just come to my mind. 'Do I have cancer like my patients?'" (Participant 18). Another participant stated, "The suffering of my patients reminds me of my deceased relatives" (Participant 17). One participant observed, "[My] inability to cope with negative emotions aroused at work may be related to [my] past unsolved bereavement experiences" (Participant 1).

Emotions participants reported experiencing in their work were a sense of helplessness and powerlessness, worry about the time constraints of death work, guilt, a sense of heaviness, being overwhelmed, and anger. For example, a participant shared his sense of helplessness and powerlessness:

> I sometimes feel powerless. I just can't do much. . . . I tried to give my patient [a] high dose of morphine, but my patient's pain was not relieved. I didn't know what to do. I felt very helpless. My patient suffered because the morphine was too heavy for my patient. . . . Not only me but also my whole palliative care team was nervous. This was stressful. I suffered as the physician. I felt helpless, just like my other colleagues in the team. (Participant 22)

Another participant also described her guilty feelings stemming from an incident at work:

It was a Friday and was getting to the end of the day. There was something I promised a patient to help with. I was thinking to leave the hospital and come back to help the coming weekend or the coming Monday. When I came back to the hospital during the weekend, my patient had already passed away. I felt sad and kept thinking that I should have helped my patient before I left on Friday and that it was my fault to leave the hospital on Friday. (Participant 1)

Existential Coping

Participants found rebuilding life and death assumptions to be a major existential coping strategy. Participants expressed their need to identify their life priorities and goals, reflect on their life, and search for the meaning of suffering and death. For example, a participant indicated her renewed life priorities and goals:

I will have a deeper thought. I will think about, to me, what my life priorities are. I keep searching my life priorities. . . . I keep thinking what things or who are the most valuable or most important to me. My meaning of life would be to do things which are most important to me and spend time with people who are most important or treasured to me. (Participant 9)

Another existential coping strategy is more action oriented: actualizing the life and death assumptions. It can be further categorized into three areas: (1) acceptance of the nature of life and death, (2) better preparation for death, and (3) living a meaningful life. The first area, acceptance of the nature of life and death, is characterized by participants' development of a revised understanding of life and death, such as suffering and regrets are inevitable in life and death cannot be controlled. For example, one participant shared, "My personal insight to life is that life and death are natural processes. Everyone has to face them. Illnesses and death are full of uncertainties. We just can't control them" (Participant 13).

The area of better preparation for death illustrates participants' willingness to face death proactively, such as enhancing their deeper understanding of death, making practical preparations for their own death, dealing with unfinished business, and discussing death openly with family members. For example, a participant shared her preparation for death:

Death is inevitable. So why don't we prepare for our death? Everyone knows that death is inevitable, ever since they are born. I rarely thought about preparing for my death before, but after I have been working in the field of palliative care, I tell myself that I have to prepare for my death. (Participant 5)

Living a meaningful life is the aspiration of the participants to live each day to the fullest by minimizing regrets, enhancing life's meaningfulness, being mindful of the present moment, fulfilling responsibilities, and being grateful for what they have. For example, a participant shared,

You have to live in the present moment. This gives you energy to face tomorrow's challenges. . . . I keep reflecting on this as you never know what will happen tomorrow. This supports me to survive and work in palliative care for six years. . . . This gives me huge encouragement. (Participant 12)

Emotional Coping

Emotional coping is categorized at both personal and professional levels. At the personal level, the coping strategies of acceptance of own emotions and management of own emotions were identified. By accepting their own emotions, participants perceived emotional arousal at death work as normal. *Management of own emotions* refers to measures to mitigate the impact of emotional arousal, such as sharing with others, relaxing, finding joy in life, rationalizing, distracting oneself by work, and dealing with losses and relationship issues. For example, one participant shared about her acceptance and management of emotions:

I have to accept that when I heard about the difficult situations of my patients or their family, I will get emotional like ordinary people do, even though I am a social work professional. . . . Because life is uncertain and unpredictable, we have to enjoy life in the present moment. (Participant 20)

At the professional level, four emotional coping methods were identified: (1) adjustment of expectations in death work, (2) searching for meaning in work, (3) differentiation between work and self, and (4) adjustment of expectations in professional identity.

Adjustment of expectations in death work may include developing suitable goals, accepting the reality of patients and families, and achieving a good death for the patient. For example, a participant stated,

> In palliative care, I aim at good death. . . . In acute care, I aim at avoiding death. . . . I have to be clear with my objective what I have to do in palliative care first. This helps regulate my negative emotions at work and reduce my emotional suffering. In palliative care, I hope to achieve a good death, or at least appropriate death. . . . This helps me adjust my emotional pathway. . . . I believe that if you as a physician aim for avoiding death in palliative care, everyone will suffer, no matter the patient or you. So I have to clarify to myself that death is unavoidable. What I have to do is to enhance the quality of the dying process. (Participant 22)

The strategy of searching for meaning in work involves participants achieving a sense of reassurance through finding meaning, satisfaction, and passion in work and experiencing love among people. A participant echoed this point: "To me, this is [the] meaning of work: The patient is touched by or change[d] positively because you have tried hard to help" (Participant 4).

The strategy of differentiation between work and self encompasses the participants' ability to separate work from personal life so that distress from work does not interfere with personal life and vice versa. It includes differentiating one's own needs or emotions from patients' needs and emotions and maintaining an optimal distance from patients.

The final strategy, adjustment of expectations in professional identity, requires participants to contemplate their professional roles and limitations. Participants revealed that it is important to acknowledge that they are not different from patients in facing death and dying, that they cannot control the fate of patients but can only be their companion, that they have to accept their own limitations as helping professionals and not take over responsibilities in patients' lives. One participant shared, "You have to strike a balance. You can't keep yourself too distanced from the patient, but you can't be too involved in your work. That means you have to separate work and personal life" (Participant 19). Another participant also acknowledged her emotions: "When a family member of my patient talked about her difficult situation, I could not help but cry. It was understandable to cry for this family member even though I am a social work professional" (Participant 20).

DISCUSSION

This study deepened the understanding of palliative care professionals' perception of the effects of death work on the self, which includes the confrontation of challenges and the development of coping skills. Echoing the previous work of W.C.H. Chan and Tin (2012) on self-competence, participants elaborated on existential and emotional concerns in relation to the self. Participants perceived their challenges of the self as both existential and emotional, and hence corresponding existential and emotional coping were developed. This study provides a more thorough elaboration of the concepts of existential and emotional challenges inherent in death work and palliative care professionals' corresponding coping strategies.

Participants identified their existential challenges as the shattering of life and death assumptions. This is similar to what people experience when they face traumatic events (Janoff-Bulman, 1989, 1992). The discrepancy between what participants experience in death work and what they believe about life and death may lead to distress and confusion. Our findings suggest that coping with this existential challenge requires rebuilding the shattered life and death assumptions. However, it seems that this rebuilding involves not only cognitive restructuring, such as rethinking life priorities, but also an action component (for example, better preparation for death) in which participants need to actualize the rebuilt assumptions of life and death. This is consistent with existential perspectives that emphasize the importance of living one's beliefs and values with courage (Camus, 1991; Frankl, 1984). A previous study on death preparation in Hong Kong also echoes this point with its finding that those who thought about preparing for their own death but did not act on those thoughts experienced higher death anxiety than did those who prepared for their own death (T.H.Y. Chan, Chan, Tin, Chow, & Chan, 2006–2007).

Our findings on emotional challenges and coping suggest that death work seems to have dual effects on the emotions of participants. At the personal level, participants' own death anxiety and grief over their losses may be aroused. At the professional level, participants' sense of guilt and helplessness may be aroused. This perhaps reveals the unique essence of death work: professional yet personal (Katz, 2006). That is the reason why coping with emotions aroused from death work should involve coping at the personal level (for example, dealing with own losses and grief) (Worden, 2002) and the professional level (for example, accepting losing control in professional practice) (Shapiro, Astin, Shapiro, Robitshek, & Shapiro, 2011).

External professional resources (for example, professional training, peer support, and supervision) are needed to support palliative care professionals (for example, social workers), especially those who are relatively inexperienced in the field of palliative and end-of-life care. We also propose that professional training focusing on the development of self-competence is an important means to effectively prepare helping professionals to cope with the existential and emotional challenges in death work.

The importance of the role of self has long been recognized in the field of social work, counseling, and psychotherapy. Freud (1917/1959), for example, believed that a successful therapist should handle his personal life to avoid becoming entangled in the patient's personal life. Bowen (1972) and Bandler, Grinder, and Satir (1976) also proposed systematic training that resolved therapists' personal conflicts from their own family of origin.

Proposals

Training models that highlight the role of self are rare in death work. To enhance the self-competence of helping professionals in death work, we propose two directions. First, helping professionals must better understand their level of competence in coping with the existential and emotional challenges in death work. Our findings on existential and emotional coping provide rich information on what is crucial when coping with these challenges. This could be a good basis for developing a scale to facilitate helping professionals' self-rating of their level of self-competence. Such awareness and understanding may be helpful for those planning to enter the field of death work.

The second direction we propose is the development of a training model to enhance helping professionals' coping skills for dealing with existential and emotional challenges in death work. On the basis of the findings of this study and our past training experience, we recommend that a training model on self-competence for death work involve the following elements.

Experiential Learning. Our findings show that the necessary coping in death work involves input coming from cognitive levels (for example, rebuilding life and death assumptions), emotional levels (for example, acceptance of own emotions), and behavioral actions (for example, actualizing the life and death assumptions). Experiential learning is therefore the most suitable means of developing helping professionals' coping strategies in death work because it is particularly effective in arousing cognitive, emotional, and behavioral changes in the learning process (Kolb, 1984).

Reflection on Own Existential and Emotional Coping in Personal Life. Helping professionals are encouraged to review their own existential and emotional coping, explore and understand how they are developing, evaluate their suitability in death work, and make any necessary changes.

Integration of Self-Competence in Professional Work. Aponte and Winter (2000) commented that existing educational models often offer an either–or model for trainees. Educational programs may focus on either professional technical skills or participants' personal growth and learning. Few programs offer an in-depth focus on both the participants' personal reflection and how such reflection relates to their professional work. We therefore propose that the training should be oriented toward not only developing the participant as a more intact person, but also supporting the participant in incorporating self-competence into technical interventions and professional work. In this way, we believe that palliative care professionals, such as social workers in palliative and end-of-life care, can then better apply "use of self" in their practice.

Limitations and Future Directions

We are aware that our participants of different disciplines may be different in their perception of challenges and adoption of coping in death work. Yet, in this study, we analyzed these data together to examine the impact of death work, the nature of work that different disciplines have in common, on the self. We plan to compare and discuss the similarities and differences between participants of different profiles (for example, different disciplines, working experience in palliative care) in future studies.

CONCLUSION

In this study, we explored how palliative care professionals perceive the impact of death work on self and how they cope with it. Existential and emotional challenges and the professionals' corresponding coping methods were revealed by the findings. Appropriate training can be developed to enhance coping with these challenges on self in death work and, in turn, enhance self-competence. **HSW**

REFERENCES

Aponte, H. J., & Winter, J. E. (2000). The person and practice of the therapist: Treatment and training. In M. Baldwin (Ed.), *The use of self in therapy* (2nd ed., pp. 127–165). New York: Haworth Press.

Bailey, C., Murphy, R., & Porock, D. (2011). Professional tears: Developing emotional intelligence around death and dying in emergency work. *Journal of Clinical Nursing, 20*, 3364–3372.

Bandler, R., Grinder, J., & Satir, V. (1976). *Changing with families: A book about further education for being human.* Palo Alto, CA: Science and Behavior Books.

Bosma, H., Johnston, M., Wainwright, W., Abernethy, N., Feron, A., Kelly, M. L., et al. (2010). Creating social work competencies for practice in hospice palliative care. *Palliative Medicine, 24*, 79–87.

Bowen, M. (1972). Toward a differentiation of a self in one's own family. In J. L. Frano (Ed.), *Family interaction: A dialogue between family researchers and family therapists* (pp. 111–173). New York: Springer.

Brandsen, C. K. (2005). Social work and palliative care: Reviewing the past and moving forward. *Journal of Social Work in End-of-Life & Palliative Care, 1*(2), 45–70.

Braun, V., & Clarke, V. (2006). Using thematic analysis in psychology. *Qualitative Research in Psychology, 3*, 77–101.

Camus, A. (1991). *The myth of Sisyphus and other essays* (J. O'Brien, Trans). New York: Random House.

Chan, T.H.Y., Chan, F.M.Y., Tin, A. F., Chow, A.Y.M., & Chan, C.L.W. (2006–2007). Death preparation and anxiety: A survey in Hong Kong. *Omega: Journal of Death and Dying, 54*, 67–78.

Chan, W.C.H. (2013). Relationships between psychosocial issues and physical symptoms of Hong Kong Chinese palliative care patients: Insights into social workers' role in symptoms management. *British Journal of Social Work, 44*, 2342–2359.

Chan, W.C.H., & Tin, A. F. (2012). Beyond knowledge and skills: Self-competence in working with death, dying, and bereavement. *Death Studies, 36*, 899–913.

Chinnery, S.-A., & Beddoe, L. (2011). Taking active steps towards the competent use of self in social work. *Advances in Social Work and Welfare Education, 13*, 127–152.

Clark, L., Leedy, S., McDonald, L., Muller, B., Lamb, C., Mendez, T., et al. (2007). Spirituality and job satisfaction among hospice interdisciplinary team members. *Journal of Palliative Medicine, 10*, 1321–1328.

Desbiens, J.-F., & Fillion, L. (2007). Coping strategies, emotional outcomes and spiritual quality of life in palliative care nurses. *International Journal of Palliative Nursing, 13*, 291–299.

Dewane, C. J. (2006). Use of self: A primer revisited. *Clinical Social Work Journal, 34*, 543–558.

Edwards, J. K., & Bess, J. M. (1998). Developing effectiveness in the therapeutic use of self. *Clinical Social Work Journal, 26*, 89–105.

Frankl, V. E. (1984). *Man's search for meaning.* New York: Pocket Books.

Freud, S. (1959). Mourning and melancholia. In J. Strachey (Ed. & Trans.), *The standard edition of the complete psychological works of Sigmund Freud* (Vol. 20, pp. 152–170). London: Hogarth Press. (Original work published 1917)

Frey, R., Gott, M., Banfield, R., & Campbell, T. (2011) What questionnaires exist to measure the perceived competence of generalists in palliative care provision? A critical literature review. *BMJ Supportive & Palliative Care, 1*, 19–32.

Gamino, L. A., & Ritter, R. H. Jr. (2012). Death competence: An ethical imperative. *Death Studies, 36*, 23–40.

Gwyther, L. P., Altilio, T., Black, S., Christ, G., Csikai, E. L., Hooyman, N., et al. (2005). Social work competencies in palliative and end-of-life care. *Journal of Social Work in End-of-Life & Palliative Care, 1*(1), 87–120.

Janoff-Bulman, R. (1989). Assumptive worlds and the stress of traumatic events: Applications of the schema construct. *Social Cognition, 7*, 113–136.

Janoff-Bulman, R. (1992). *Shattered assumptions: Towards a new psychology of trauma.* New York: Free Press.

Katz, R. S. (2006). When our personal selves influence our professional work: An introduction to emotions and countertransference in end-of-life care. In R. S. Katz & T. A. Johnson (Eds.), *When professionals weep* (pp. 3–12). New York: Routledge.

Keene, E. A., Hutton, N., Hall, B., & Rushton, C. (2010). Bereavement debriefing sessions: An intervention to support health care professionals in managing their grief after the death of a patient. *Pediatric Nursing, 36*, 185–189.

Kolb, D. (1984). *Experiential learning: Experience as the source of learning and development.* Englewood Cliffs, NJ: Prentice Hall.

Lynch, T., Connor, S., & Clark, D. (2013). Mapping levels of palliative care development: A global update. *Journal of Pain and Symptom Management, 45*, 1094–1106.

Melvin, C. S. (2012). Professional compassion fatigue: What is the true cost of nurses caring for the dying? *International Journal of Palliative Nursing, 18*, 606–611.

Meo, N., Hwang, U., & Morrison, R. S. (2011). Resident perceptions of palliative care training in the emergency department. *Journal of Palliative Medicine, 14*, 548–555.

Patton, M. Q. (1999). Enhancing the quality and credibility of qualitative analysis. *Health Services Research, 34*, 1189–1208.

Payne, N. (2001). Occupational stressors and coping as determinants of burnout in female hospice nurses. *Journal of Advanced Nursing, 33*, 396–405.

Pereira, S. M., Fonseca, A. M., & Carvalho, A. S. (2011). Burnout in palliative care: A systematic review. *Nursing Ethics, 18*, 317–326.

Peters, L., Cant, R., Sellick, K., O'Connor, M., Lee, S., & Burney, S. (2012). Is work stress in palliative care nurses a cause for concern? A literature review. *International Journal of Palliative Nursing, 18*, 561–567.

Prochnau, C., Liu, L., & Boman, J. (2003). Personal–professional connections in palliative care occupational therapy. *American Journal of Occupational Therapy, 57*, 196–204.

Richards, L. (2015). *Handling qualitative data: A practical guide.* Los Angeles: Sage Publications.

Sanchez-Reilly, S., Morrison, L., Carey, E., Bernacki, R., O'Neill, L., Kapo, J., et al. (2013). Caring for oneself to care for others: Physicians and their self-care. *Journal of Supportive Oncology, 11*, 75–81.

Shapiro, J., Astin, J., Shapiro, S. L., Robitshek, D., & Shapiro, D. H. (2011). Coping with loss of control in the practice of medicine. *Families, Systems, & Health, 29*, 15–28.

Sinclair, S. (2011). Impact of death and dying on the personal lives and practices of palliative and hospice care professionals. *Canadian Medical Association Journal, 183*, 180–187.

Slocum-Gori, S., Hemsworth, D., Chan, W. W., Carson, A., & Kazanjian, A. (2013). Understanding compassion satisfaction, compassion fatigue and burnout: A survey of the hospice palliative care workforce. *Palliative Medicine, 27*, 172–178.

Steven, A., White, G., & Marples, G. (2014). Enhancing confidence and competence in end of life care: An educational pathway for community nursing staff. *BMJ Supportive & Palliative Care, 4*(Suppl. 1), A36.

Tong, A., Sainsbury, P., & Craig, J. (2007). Consolidated criteria for reporting qualitative research (COREQ): A 32-item checklist for interviews and focus groups. *International Journal for Quality in Health Care, 19,* 349–357.

Worden, J. W. (2002). *Grief counseling and grief therapy: A handbook for the mental health practitioner* (3rd ed.). New York: Springer.

Zambrano, S. C., Chur-Hansen, A., & Crawford, G. B. (2014). The experiences, coping mechanisms, and impact of death and dying on palliative medicine specialists. *Palliative and Supportive Care, 12*, 309–316.

Wallace Chi Ho Chan, PhD, RSW, FT, is assistant professor, Department of Social Work, Chinese University of Hong Kong, Shatin, 852 h Hong Kong 96689770; e-mail: chchan@swk.cuhk.edu.hk. *Agnes Fong, MSW, RSW, FT,* is honorary lecturer, Centre on Behavioral Health, University of Hong Kong. *Karen Lok Yi Wong, MA,* was research assistant, Department of Social Work, Chinese University of Hong Kong. *Doris Man Wah Tse, MBBS (HK), FHKCP, FHKAM (Med.), FRCP (Lond.), FRCP (Edin.),* is hospital chief executive, Caritas Medical Centre, Hong Kong. *Kam Shing Lau, MBBS (HK), FRCP (Edin.), FHKCP, FHKAM (Med.),* is chief of service (integrated medical service), Ruttonjee and Tang Shiu Kin Hospitals, Hong Kong. *Lai Ngor Chan, RN, RGN, RM,* is department operation manager, Pulmonary and Palliative Care, Haven of Hope Hospital, Hong Kong. This research is funded by the General Research Fund, the Research Grants Council of the Hong Kong Special Administrative Region, China (Project No.: CUHK 441511).

Original manuscript received December 5, 2014
Final revision received January 9, 2015
Accepted January 20, 2015
Advance Access Publication November 27, 2015

GIVE US YOUR POINT OF VIEW!

Viewpoint submissions, which go through the normal peer review process, should be no longer than seven double-spaced pages. Send your Viewpoint column as a Word document through the online portal at http://hsw.msubmit.net (initial, one-time registration is required).

CAREGIVING AND CARE SHARING
A LIFE COURSE PERSPECTIVE
ROBERTA R. GREENE AND NANCY P. KROPF

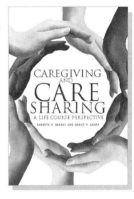

Caregiving and care sharing take place across the life course and involve various configurations. Although there are similarities, families have different needs and experiences of care depending on the caregiving situation, life course issues, and unique personal history.

In *Caregiving and Care Sharing: A Life Course Perspective*, the authors highlight the experience of providing care in several different family situations. This book not only serves as a guide to assist those caring for older adults, but also examines the experiences of older caregivers caring for younger adults, as older parents care for adult children with intellectual and psychiatric conditions, or when grandparents are raising their grandchildren. The caregiving needs of veterans are also addressed.

ISBN: 978-0-87101-456-6. 2014.
Item #4566. 272 pages. $47.99.
1-800-227-3590 • www.naswpress.org

NASW PRESS

CODE APCC15

Traumatic Exposure History as a Risk Factor for Chronic Pain in Adult Patients with Sickle Cell Disease

Teresa Works, Sasia Jones, James Grady, and Biree Andemariam

This article describes the impact of the integration of a licensed clinical social worker (LCSW) with expertise in behavioral health on identification of risk factors for chronic pain in a cohort of adults with sickle cell disease. Authors conducted a retrospective chart review of all visits to the adult sickle cell center during the first six months of LCSW integration. Demographics, clinical history, and LCSW notes were reviewed. Overall, 71 patients were introduced to the LCSW; 55 percent of them had chronic pain. Patients with chronic pain were older, used opioids daily, took hydroxyurea, reported higher daily pain scores, and underwent more acute care visits and hospitalizations for pain with longer stays. Fifty-eight (81 percent) patients requested concrete social work services such as transportation and housing. Thirty-two patients (55 percent) expressed a desire for mental health counseling while receiving concrete services. Twenty-two (69 percent) of these patients self-disclosed at least one traumatic experience. In fact, a statistically significant relationship between chronic pain and a history of trauma was identified ($p = 0.001$). Results suggest that sickle cell patients should receive clinical social work services to assess for traumatic exposures that may influence chronic pain.

KEY WORDS: *chronic pain; LCSWs; sickle cell disease; trauma*

The biopsychosocial philosophy of clinical care means that to respond appropriately to patient pain and suffering, clinicians must deal with all of the dimensions of the illness (Borrell-Carrió, Suchman, & Epstein, 2004; Engel, 1981; Gitterman & Rovinelli, 2011). This includes the psychological, social, and environmental dimensions of care as well as the physical manifestations of disease. An ecological approach to clinical care consists of provider focus on the "goodness of fit" between a person and his or her environment (Gitterman & Rovinelli, 2011). Clinical social workers who integrate biopsychosocial and ecological approaches to care are uniquely suited to working with people suffering from chronic diseases such as sickle cell disease (SCD). Their unique skill set allows them to assess and intervene on the multiple and often complex issues that affect a person's sense of wellness and health.

Approximately one in 500 African Americans are born with SCD, an inherited hematological disorder (Hollins et al., 2012). In SCD, hemoglobin-containing red blood cells form an irregular "sickled" shape and occlude small blood vessels, causing intense acute pain, organ dysfunction, and early mortality (Platt, 2008). Acute vaso-occlusive pain episodes are the hallmark of SCD and the primary cause of hospitalizations in this patient population. These unpredictable episodes of severe pain may be precipitated by a number of triggers such as hypoxia, dehydration, and infection (Ballas, Gupta, & Adams-Graves, 2012; Casey, Greenberg, Nicassio, Harpin, & Hubbard, 2008; Citero et al., 2007; Horsham & Chung, 2013; Hunt & Alisky, 2013; PTSD Alliance, n.d.; Unal, Toros, Kutuk, & Uyaniker, 2011), yet exact mechanisms leading to the onset of pain remain unknown.

Although pain in SCD is mostly regarded as an episodic phenomenon, up to 44 percent of patients develop chronic pain (Ballas et al., 2006). Similar to acute SCD pain, the genesis of chronic pain is uncertain. There is little research on the etiology of chronic pain in SCD; however, it does appear to develop in individuals who have had more frequent acute pain episodes, central nervous system changes, avascular necrosis, and chronic osteomyelitis or ankle ulcers (Ballas et al., 2012). Pharmacological therapy of chronic pain remains the mainstay, with high-dose long-acting opioid-based therapy and antineuropathic pain treatments most commonly prescribed (Ballas, 2011; Jacob & American Pain Society, 2001).

The role of behavioral therapy in the treatment of chronic pain in SCD has been impeded by a dearth of literature exploring the relationship between chronic pain and comorbid mental health challenges in this population. Although depression and anxiety have been studied among cohorts of SCD patients, to our knowledge there has not been any published work examining the relationship between traumatic exposure and chronic pain in this population (Edwards et al., 2005; Levenson et al., 2008; Sogutlu, Levenson, McClish, Rosef, & Smith, 2011). This is particularly surprising in light of us knowing that of the estimated 70 percent of adults in the general U.S. population who have experienced a traumatic event at least once in their lives, up to 20 percent go on to develop posttraumatic stress disorder (PTSD Alliance, n.d.). In fact, a relationship between traumatic exposure and chronic pain in non-SCD-related illnesses has been established (Casey et al., 2008). Cumulative traumatic life events have also been found to be linked to the increased severity of subsequent pain in non-SCD disorders (Casey et al., 2008). Yet the influence of traumatic exposure on chronic pain in SCD has not been explored.

The purpose of our study was to examine the relationship between demographic factors, clinical history, and traumatic exposure on the presence of chronic pain in adult patients with SCD as identified through the integration of a social worker with behavioral health expertise into a comprehensive SCD management team.

METHOD
Study Population and Setting
The New England Sickle Cell Institute at University of Connecticut Health (UConn Health), the only adult comprehensive SCD program in the northern region of Connecticut, was established in 2009. Initially, the center was staffed by a hematologist, a nurse practitioner, and a registered nurse. Patients underwent full medical evaluations and participated in the development of comprehensive treatment plans. Social and emotional barriers to treatment were identified; however, resources to manage the identified barriers were limited by a lack of expertise. Therefore, a full-time licensed clinical social worker (LCSW) with expertise in medical social work and behavioral health was integrated into the team framework in 2012 to identify and address social and emotional barriers to clinical care.

Thereafter, the LCSW met with each patient during his or her comprehensive medical visit and offered both concrete and clinical social work services. Utilization of the LCSW's services was at the discretion of the patient. The social worker used these visits to engage the patients to optimize treatment. Concrete social work services included assistance with transportation, housing, social services entitlements, legal issues, utilities, and affordable medications. Clinical services included one-on-one behavioral health therapy sessions focusing on emotional symptom reduction such as treatment of depression and anxiety, assistance with coping with chronic and acute phases of illness, and family therapy.

Study Design
This study was undertaken in accordance with UConn Health's institutional review board standards. We conducted a retrospective chart review of all consecutive patients with SCD who presented for comprehensive medical evaluation during the first six months that the LCSW was integrated into the adult SCD center. Charts were reviewed for demographic factors (gender, age, race, and insurance type) and clinical information (genotype, average daily pain score, opioid utilization, presence of avascular necrosis, number of presentations and hospitalizations for vaso-occlusive pain crisis episodes, hydroxyurea use, and chronic transfusion therapy). Patients were categorized as having chronic pain if they self-reported having pain more than 50 percent of days for six months or more. LCSW records and medical charts were reviewed for the number and specific types of traumatic experiences and encounters disclosed by patients.

In this study, a *traumatic experience* was defined as witnessing or being threatened with an event that involves actual injury, a threat to the physical integrity of one's self or others, or possible death. Patients were categorized as trauma exposed based on their reaction to traumatic encounters (intense fear, helplessness, horror, or emotional shock). Any patient who was exposed to a traumatic event and responded to the event with intense fear, helplessness, horror, or emotional shock was considered to have a history of trauma exposure and was categorized as such. A patient may have been exposed to one or more events but did not have a response to the event or documented evidence of a response. These patients were not considered to be trauma exposed.

Statistical Analysis

All statistical analyses were performed using IBM SPSS Version 21 (IBM Corp., 2012). Pearson's chi-square test was used to assess associations among categorical variables. When the assumptions of the chi-square test were not met, Fisher's exact test was used instead. For continuous variables that satisfied all of the requisite assumptions, differences in group means were assessed using unpaired two-sample t tests. Those that did not satisfy the assumption of population normality were instead analyzed using the nonparametric Wilcoxon rank-sum test.

RESULTS

Population Characteristics

A total of 71 consecutive unique patients with SCD presented for comprehensive medical evaluation over the first six months of LCSW integration into the care team (see Table 1). The mean age of the patients was 31 years. A majority of the patients were black and had the SS hemoglobin phenotype of SCD. More than half of these patients had chronic pain.

Table 1: Population Characteristics ($N = 71$)

Characteristic	n	%
Gender		
Male	32	45
Female	39	55
Race/ethnicity		
Black	65	92
Latino	5	7
White	1	1
Insurance		
Private	15	21
Medicaid	35	49
Medicare	21	30
Age (years)		
18–24	35	49
25–34	19	27
35–44	10	14
45–54	7	10
Genotype		
SS	47	66
SC	12	17
Sβ^+	9	13
Sβ^0	3	4
Chronic pain		
Yes	39	55
No	32	45
Used social work services		
Yes	58	82
No	13	13

During the introduction to the LCSW, 82 percent of patients verbalized a desire for concrete social work services (see Table 2). The two types of concrete social work services most commonly used were (1) health management and compliance and (2) transportation. Health management and compliance services included working with a patient to identify and eliminate barriers to taking medications and attending medical appointments, and reinforcing positive skills needed to follow medical advice. These services included patient referral to the Department of Social Services and identification of low-cost medication formularies. Transportation-related services included completing paperwork for medical cabs or paratransit (public transportation for those with disabilities), assisting with calls for a medical cab, and providing cab vouchers or bus tokens. Fifty-three percent of patients required more than one type of concrete service. Nearly one-fifth of patients worked with the LCSW on at least three different concrete services.

Thirty-two (55 percent) of the patients expressed a need for mental health counseling to the LCSW. These patients began one-on-one therapy sessions with the LCSW. It is notable that no patients opted for mental health counseling during the initial interaction with the LCSW. All requests for counseling evolved over the course of working with the LCSW in the context of concrete services.

Identification of Traumatic Exposures through LCSW Patient Counseling

Twenty-two (69 percent) out of the 32 patients who began one-on-one therapy sessions self-disclosed a

Table 2: Utilization of Social Work Services ($N = 71$)

Service	n	%
Concrete services	58	82
Categories[a]		
Health management/compliance		48
Transportation		29
Information and referral		24
Housing		14
Social services entitlement		14
Vocational/educational		10
Legal issues		7
Utilities and affordable medications		7
Clinical services[b]	32	55

[a]Percentage of patients using the listed categories of concrete services offered by the licensed clinical social worker. Some patients used more than one concrete service and are represented in more than one category.
[b]All patients who received clinical services were among the 58 patients who received concrete services.

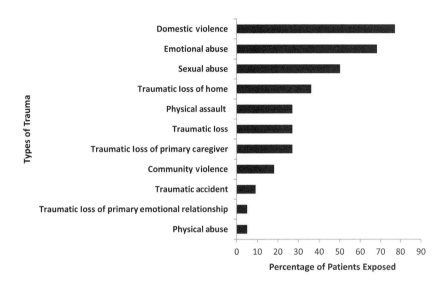

Figure 1: Traumatic Exposures Reported by Trauma-Affected Patients Receiving Clinical Services

personal history of traumatic exposure during a counseling session. Although all 22 patients identified their SCD, severe episodes of acute illness, or poor care from medical providers as traumatic, each patient also disclosed at least one other traumatic exposure, as indicated in Figure 1. All 22 patients were exposed to more than one type of trauma, with the most common being domestic violence, emotional abuse, and sexual abuse. The median number of types of traumatic exposures in this cohort was five. Only one patient had previously received mental health counseling. Eighty-six percent of the patients with a traumatic exposure history also had chronic pain.

Risk Factors for Chronic Pain

Risk factors for the presence of chronic pain were evaluated in the entire cohort of 71 patients (see Table 3). Chronic pain was not influenced by gender or type of insurance. Older age was significantly associated with chronic pain. Hemoglobin genotype, the presence of avascular necrosis, and the need for chronic transfusion therapy did not appear to influence chronic pain. Individuals with chronic pain were more likely to use daily opioid medications, have a higher daily pain score, and use hydroxyurea. They made twice as many acute visits for pain management. They were also more likely to require hospitalization for vaso-occlusive crisis pain episodes and, when admitted, to have a longer median hospitalization (eight versus five days). Individuals with chronic pain were significantly more likely to have disclosed a history of traumatic experience.

DISCUSSION

Our study has identified both expected and unexpected risk factors for chronic pain in adults with SCD. Indeed, we found a significant relationship between the presence of chronic pain and older age, higher daily pain scores, the need for daily opioids, and greater acute care utilization. Patients with chronic pain were more frequent users of care for acute pain episodes both in the emergency department and in the SCD clinic. This pattern of utilization likely influenced the higher number of hospitalizations for acute pain. It is intriguing to postulate that chronic pain itself played a role in these utilization patterns and the longer hospitalizations, particularly because there remains no objective way to discriminate acute from chronic pain. The fact that patients with chronic pain were more likely to be prescribed hydroxyurea is also not surprising and possibly relates to the fact that these patients also had a greater number of acute pain episodes. Hydroxyurea itself is not known to have an effect on the amelioration of chronic pain but is indicated for the prevention of frequent acute painful episodes in adults with SCD (Charache et al., 1995).

Table 3: Risk Factor Analysis for Chronic Pain

	Chronic Pain		
	Yes	No	p Value
Demographics			
Gender, n (%)			
Female	23 (59)	16 (41)	
Male	16 (50)	16 (50)	NS
Insurance, n (%)			
Private	6 (40)	9 (60)	
Medicaid	18 (51)	17 (49)	
Medicare	15 (71)	6 (29)	NS
Age, in years, M (SD)	34 (10)	29 (8)	0.03
Clinical factors			
Genotype, n (%)			
SS	27 (57)	20 (43)	
SC	6 (50)	6 (50)	
Sβ^+	6 (67)	3 (33)	
Sβ^0	0 (0)	3 (100)	NS
Daily opioid use, n (%)			
Yes	36 (97)	1 (3)	
No	3 (9)	31 (91)	<0.0001
Average daily pain score, M (SD)	5 (3)	2 (3)	<0.0001
Avascular necrosis, n (%)			
Yes	9 (64)	5 (36)	
No	30 (53)	27 (47)	NS
Chronic transfusion therapy, n (%)			
Yes	18 (67)	9 (33)	
No	21 (48)	23 (52)	NS
Hydroxyurea utilization, n (%)			
Yes	18 (72)	7 (28)	
No	21 (46)	25 (54)	0.03
VOC episodes requiring hospitalization, Mdn (IQR)[a]	1 (0,7)	0 (0,1)	0.004
LOS for VOC episodes requiring hospitalization, days, Mdn (IQR)	8 (6,15)	5 (4,8)	0.02
Acute care visits for VOC episodes, Mdn (IQR)[a,b]	4 (2,16)	2 (0,4)	0.007
Mental health factors			
History of traumatic experience, n (%)			
Yes	20 (83)	4 (17)	
No	19 (40)	28 (60)	0.001

Notes: NS = not significant; VOC = vaso-occlusive crisis; IQR = intra-quartile range; LOS = length of stay (days).
[a]Data were missing from five patients and include one year of VOC episodes just prior to the integration of the licensed clinical social worker into the clinical practice.
[b]Includes visits for VOC episodes to either the emergency department or the sickle cell clinic.

A few findings were unexpected. We expected that patients with chronic pain would be more likely to have avascular necrosis, a complication present in up to 87 percent of adults with SCD due to a lack of blood flow to bone resulting in bone collapse, destruction, and pain (Hernigou, Bachir, & Galacteros, 2003). We also hypothesized that patients with generally more severe genotypes (SS and Sβ0) would be more likely to have chronic pain due to more frequent episodes of acute pain and secondary complications. However, there was no relationship between chronic pain and genotype or avascular necrosis in our cohort. This suggests that chronic pain may indeed be influenced by factors other than repeated episodes of vaso-occlusion.

One of the key findings in our study was the identification of traumatic exposure as a risk factor for the presence of chronic pain. Although some studies have looked at self-reports of daily stress in individuals with SCD and chronic pain, these studies did not specifically evaluate the relationship between traumatic exposure and chronic pain (Dampier et al., 2011; Gil, Carson, Porter, Scipio, & Bediako, 2004; McClish et al., 2005; Porter et al., 1998). We were struck by both the number and types of traumatic exposures endured by our patients. The fact that only one patient had ever received formal counseling was revealing and underscores the need for more psychosocial support in what appears to be a trauma-vulnerable population. We believe that the integration of an LCSW with experience in mental health counseling and the biopsychosocial and ecological models of care into our management of adults with SCD was critical to our ability to elucidate this relationship. It is important to note that our findings could set the basis for further investigation, including a longitudinal analysis of the temporal relationship between traumatic exposure and chronic pain onset as well as the impact of mental health counseling on chronic pain management.

In general, there is a high likelihood of exposure to traumatic events over the course of a lifetime. The literature examining the prevalence of trauma suggests that at least two-thirds of U.S. adults have experienced at least one traumatic event (Resnick, Kilpatrick, Dansky, Saunders, & Best, 1993). It appears that patients with SCD may have a higher rate of traumatic exposure than the average population. This may be, in part, due to the nature of SCD, its acute pain crises, as well as the frequency of contact with the medical system, all of which can be traumatic experiences for patients. The longer one lives with SCD, the more likely one is to have complications related to the disease that may biologically influence the development of chronic pain. It is therefore possible that traumatic exposure and the development of chronic pain are both a manifestation of aging rather than directly influencing each other. In addition, the fact that many patients with SCD are African American places the population at an increased vulnerability to trauma exposure and its effects (Resnick et al., 1993). Numerous studies have linked injustice, discrimination, and health care disparities with an immense range of psychological and physical abnormalities. Injustice for patients with chronic pain leads to more pain, stress, and disability related to their condition (Zempsky, 2009, 2010).

Patients with SCD often struggle with issues of marginalization and stigma due, in part, to negative interactions with medical professionals (Haywood et al., 2014; Zempsky, 2010). Our study further validates these findings through self-reports of traumatic experiences related to medical encounters for the treatment of crisis pain. In fact, frequent injustices experienced through interactions with the health care system coupled with helplessness and the lack of control experienced by patients with SCD may serve to worsen their fragile health (Zempsky, 2009). From the patient standpoint, interactions with the health care system can perpetuate mistrust and feelings of mistreatment by medical professionals. Patients report medical staff being preoccupied with patient drug addiction and inadequate analgesic administration. They also report a lack of empathy to their reports of pain (Zempsky, 2009).

In the non-SCD population, a number of studies have demonstrated that multiple exposures to traumatic events, whether occurring within the same type of event or across event types, are associated with higher levels of physical and mental health symptoms. A study that screened and evaluated women in primary care settings for sexual and physical abuse found that childhood abuse was associated with higher levels of physical symptoms and psychological distress (depression, anxiety, somatization, and low self-esteem) (McCauley et al., 1997). These women were also more likely to have had a psychiatric admission, abuse substances, and attempt suicide. In the SCD population, several studies have indicated a strong relationship between daily pain, stress, and mood. These studies have demonstrated that increased stress and negative mood are associated with higher reported daily pain levels (Dampier et al., 2011; Edwards et al., 2005; Gil et al., 2004; Levenson et al., 2008; Porter et al., 1998). Studies in patients with SCD have also found associations between daily increases in stress and decreases in school, work, and social activities and also increases in health care utilization (Gil et al., 2004). In addition, anxiety and depression are common among patients with SCD at rates similar to those found among those suffering from other chronic and serious medical disorders (Levenson et al., 2008). Patients with SCD experience a severely compromised health-related quality of life (HRQoL), similar to that of patients receiving hemodialysis, yet the impact of traumatic exposure on HRQoL among patients with SCD has not yet been explored (McClish et al., 2005).

It is important to note that our study revealed that over half of our patients expressed a desire for mental health counseling while undergoing concrete services. Sixty-nine percent of these patients self-disclosed at least one traumatic experience, and most identified multiple types of traumatic events. Given that the trauma exposures were spontaneous disclosures by patients, a more deliberate and thorough trauma screening process may have elicited an even higher number of lifetime traumatic exposures. For that reason, we postulate that the number of traumatic exposures disclosed in this cohort represents an underestimate of the true trauma burden.

Understanding the impact and true burden of trauma in patients with SCD may lead to an improvement in the overall quality of care in the SCD community. Because there appeared, in our cohort, to be a relationship between traumatic exposure and chronic pain, the role of the clinical social worker remains vital in a comprehensive SCD clinic. Integrating a social worker into a comprehensive SCD clinic needs to be understood as a process. It is difficult for most people to ask for help regardless of whether they live with a chronic disease. Ideally, social workers should engage individuals with SCD frequently, and especially during times that they are feeling physically at their best. Social workers need to be able to understand that there is an opportunity to engage patients and establish a therapeutic relationship over time while performing concrete services tasks.

Most patients in our study did not spontaneously disclose trauma initially. Only when patients had the opportunity to have their basic needs met, in addition to the opportunity to get to know the social worker, was the disclosure of trauma made. Having a social worker using a biopsychosocial and ecological approach as a part of the comprehensive clinical team is critical. The social worker can assess patients' overall well-being in regard to work, school, relationships, and potential barriers in care. If issues are identified, the social worker can then establish how he or she can help. We believe that adoption of a biopsychosocial and ecological treatment framework contributed to the development of therapeutic alliances between the social worker and patients. These trust-based alliances likely influenced patient comfort in spontaneously disclosing traumatic experiences. Patients likely saw the clinical social worker as a resource to their overall well-being, which allowed for assessment of other psychosocial factors that may exacerbate pain and other disease complications. This approach might lead to clinical practice interventions (such as managing traumatic events proactively) with at-risk chronic disease patients to avoid additional exacerbation of medical complications such as the development of chronic pain. Meeting with patients with SCD when they come for regular transfusions or outpatient clinic appointments can present engagement and assistance opportunities. Patients may report impediments such as transportation issues, loss of insurance or entitlements, and housing issues that could contribute to an impaired ability to follow treatment recommendations. When patients become aware that their social worker genuinely cares about them and could be of great assistance, a therapeutic alliance begins to form. Frequent contact between the patient and the social worker also contributes to the establishment of trust. A therapeutic alliance between a social worker and a patient opens the opportunity for discussions to become more clinical in nature. The social worker can then assess for traumatic exposures or other stressors that may exacerbate the perception of pain. The offering of concrete services in our cohort led to the development of a therapeutic alliance between the patient and the social worker, allowing for the screening and identification of traumatic exposures. This will hopefully lead to better outcomes as they relate to the care and treatment of chronic pain.

Limitations of this study include the fact that the study was retrospective and relied on patients' self-disclosure of their trauma history. A more robust sample and prospective systematic screening of patients for traumatic exposure and onset of chronic pain would be valuable. This study included a cohort of patients who were introduced to the social worker during the first six months of her integration into the SCD care team. Therefore, patients may not have been clear on the scope of practice that the clinical social worker could provide, possibly making them less likely to engage in either concrete or clinical services. Although our cohort of patients was demographically and clinically similar to other adult SCD populations, there are inherent limits to the generalizability of our findings. Most notable is the fact that our adult SCD program has a full-time social worker with expertise in the management of comorbid mental health disorders. Our social worker's expertise may have increased the level of comfort that our patients experienced, which may have translated into an increased willingness to disclose very painful histories. Our study is also limited in that we did not include children and have not followed individuals longitudinally to better elucidate the effect of aging and cumulative traumatic exposures on the contemporaneous development of chronic pain. Nonetheless, our study demonstrates a very high prevalence of traumatic exposures in our patients with SCD, which suggests that the SCD population as a whole may be at particular risk.

Because the integration of an LCSW into our care team allowed us to ascertain the presence of trauma exposure in our patients with SCD, we suggest that clinical social work should be integrated as a fundamental part of care. A clinically trained social worker is ideal for both identifying and treating trauma and its emotional and physical impact on SCD pain. Often, individuals with SCD do not have a social worker available to them. Despite the fact that multiple organizations, including the National Institutes of Health and the American Pain Society, have published guidelines recommending a multidisciplinary approach to treating patients with SCD, mental health care is not always an integral component in comprehensive SCD clinics (Benjamin, Jacox, Odesina, & More, 1999; National Institutes of Health, National Heart, Lung, and Blood Institute, 2002). Mental health issues often coexist with pain syndromes and should be treated simultaneously for optimal disease management. Addressing emotional symptoms and identifying trauma history in patients early could reduce the prevalence of chronic pain syndromes in patients with SCD. Clinical social workers must be aware of both micro- and macro-level pain and trauma issues that patients with SCD may present to better intervene on both individual and system levels of care. Incorporating mental health care as a component of comprehensive care not only improves the quality of care for patients with SCD, but also opens possibilities for the development of nonpharmacologic coping skills, which in turn may reduce patient dependence on opioids and other adjunctive analgesics. Improvement of the quality of care in this approach has the potential to improve both disease and symptom management, which may in turn lead to an increase in the quality of life experienced by patients with SCD. Mental health treatment can focus on the reduction of trauma symptoms and the resolution of traumatic events. In addition, coping with stress and the management of anxiety secondary to traumatic exposure may prevent the development of chronic pain syndrome going forward.

More research is clearly needed to further explore the relationship between SCD, traumatic life events, and the development of chronic pain, and also to study the impact of behavioral health therapy on chronic pain management in those with traumatic exposures. Clinical social workers are key to the development of this body of knowledge as they are often working with the most chronically ill patients and tasked with assessing all of their biopsychosocial needs. **HSW**

REFERENCES

Ballas, S. K. (2011). Update on pain management in sickle cell disease. *Hemoglobin, 35*, 520–529. doi:10.3109/03630269.2011.610478

Ballas, S. K., Barton, F. B., Waclawiw, M. A., Swerdlow, P., Eckman, J. R., Pegelow, C. H., et al. (2006). Hydroxyurea and sickle cell anemia: Effect on quality of life. *Health and Quality of Life Outcomes, 4*, 59.

Ballas, S. K., Gupta, K., & Adams-Graves, P. (2012). Sickle cell pain: A critical reappraisal. *Blood, 120*, 3647–3656. doi:10.1182/blood-2012-04-383430

Benjamin, L., Jacox, D., Odesina, A., & More, N. (1999). *Guideline for the management of acute and chronic pain in sickle-cell disease*. Chicago: American Pain Society.

Borrell-Carrió, F., Suchman, A., & Epstein, R. (2004). The biopsychosocial model 25 years later: Principles, practice, and scientific inquiry. *Annals of Family Medicine, 2*, 576–582.

Casey, C. Y., Greenberg, M. A., Nicassio, P. M., Harpin, R. E., & Hubbard, D. (2008). Transition from acute to chronic pain and disability: A model including cognitive, affective, and trauma factors. *Pain, 134*(1–2), 69–79.

Charache, S., Terrin, M. L., Moore, R. D., Dover, G. J., Barton, F. B., Eckert, S. V., et al. (1995). Effect of hydroxyurea on the frequency of painful crises in sickle cell anemia: Investigators of the multicenter study of hydroxyurea in sickle cell anemia. *New England Journal of Medicine, 332*, 1317–1322. doi:10.1056/NEJM199505183322001

Citero, V. de A., Levenson, J. L., McClish, D. K., Bovbjerg, V. E., Cole, P. L., Dahman, B. A., et al. (2007). The role of catastrophizing in sickle cell disease—the PiSCES project. *Pain, 133*(1–3), 39–46.

Dampier, C., LeBeau, P., Rhee, S., Lieff, S., Kesler, K., Ballas, S., et al. (2011). Health-related quality of life in adults with sickle cell disease (SCD): A report from the Comprehensive Sickle Cell Centers Clinical Trial Consortium. *American Journal of Hematology, 86*(2), 203–205. doi:10.1002/ajh.21905

Edwards, C. L., Scales, M. T., Loughlin, C., Bennett, G. G., Harris-Peterson, S., De Castro, L. M., et al. (2005). A brief review of the pathophysiology, associated pain, and psychosocial issues in sickle cell disease. *International Journal of Behavioral Medicine, 12*(3), 171–179. doi:10.1207/s15327558ijbm1203_6

Engel, G. L. (1981). The clinical application of the biopsychosocial model. *Journal of Medicine and Philosophy, 6*(2), 101–124. doi:10.1093/jmp/6.2.101

Gil, K., Carson, J., Porter, L., Scipio, C., & Bediako, S. (2004). Daily mood and stress predict pain, health care use, and work activity in African American adults with sickle-cell disease. *Health Psychology, 23*, 267–274.

Gitterman, A., & Rovinelli, N. (2011). Integrating social work perspectives and models with concepts, methods and skills with other professions' specialized approaches. *Clinical Social Work Journal, 39*(2), 204–211.

Haywood, C. Jr., Diener-West, M., Strouse, J., Carroll, C. P., Bediako, S., Lanzkron, S., et al. (2014). Perceived discrimination in health care is associated with a greater burden of pain in sickle cell disease. *Journal of Pain and Symptom Management, 48*, 934–43. doi:10.1016/j.jpainsymman.2014.02.002

Hernigou, P., Bachir, D., & Galacteros, F. (2003). The natural history of symptomatic osteonecrosis in adults with sickle-cell disease. *Journal of Bone and Joint Surgery: American Volume, 85-A*, 500–504.

Hollins, M., Stonerock, G. L., Kisaalita, N. R., Jones, S., Orringer, E., & Gil, K. M. (2012). Detecting the emergence of chronic pain in sickle cell disease.

Journal of Pain and Symptom Management, 43, 1082–1093. doi:10.1016/j.jpainsymman.2011.06.020

Horsham, S., & Chung, M. C. (2013). Investigation of the relationship between trauma and pain catastrophising: The roles of emotional processing and altered self-capacity. *Psychiatry Research, 208*(3), 274–284. doi:10.1016/j.psychres.2012.11.031

Hunt, S., & Alisky, J. (2013). Inpatient management of sickle cell disease. *Hospital Medicine Clinics, 2*, e247–e262.

IBM Corp. (2012). IBM SPSS (Version 21) [Computer software]. Armonk, NY: Author.

Jacob, E., & American Pain Society. (2001). Pain management in sickle cell disease. *Pain Management Nursing, 2*(4), 121–131. doi:10.1053/jpmn.2001.26297

Levenson, J. L., McClish, D. K., Dahman, B. A., Bovbjerg, V. E., Citero, V. de A., Penberthy, L. T., et al. (2008). Depression and anxiety in adults with sickle cell disease: The PiSCES project. *Psychosomatic Medicine, 70*(2), 192–196. doi:10.1097/PSY.0b013e31815ff5c5

McCauley, J., Kern, D. E., Kolodner, K., Dill, L., Schroeder, A. F., DeChant, H. K., et al. (1997). Clinical characteristics of women with a history of childhood abuse: Unhealed wounds. *JAMA, 277*, 1362–1368.

McClish, D., Penberthy, L., Bovbjerg, V., Roberts, J., Aisiku, I., Levenson, J., et al. (2005). Health related quality of life in sickle cell patients: The PiSCES project. *Health and Quality of Life Outcomes, 3*, 50–56.

National Institutes of Health, National Heart, Lung, and Blood Institute. (2002). *The management of sickle cell disease* (NIH Publication No. 02–2117; 4th ed.). Bethesda, MD: Author.

Platt, O. S. (2008). Hydroxyurea for the treatment of sickle cell anemia. *New England Journal of Medicine, 358*, 1362–1369. doi:10.1056/NEJMct0708272

Porter, L. S., Gil, K. M., Sedway, J. A., Ready, J., Workman, E., & Thompson, R. J. Jr. (1998). Pain and stress in sickle cell disease: An analysis of daily pain records. *International Journal of Behavioral Medicine, 5*(3), 185–203. doi:10.1207/s15327558ijbm0503_1

PTSD Alliance. (n.d.). *What is posttraumatic stress disorder?* Retrieved from http://www.ptsdalliance.org/about_what.html

Resnick, H. S., Kilpatrick, D. G., Dansky, B. S., Saunders, B. E., & Best, C. L. (1993). Prevalence of civilian trauma and posttraumatic stress disorder in a representative national sample of women. *Journal of Consulting and Clinical Psychology, 61*, 984–991.

Sogutlu, A., Levenson, J. L., McClish, D. K., Rosef, S. D., & Smith, W. R. (2011). Somatic symptom burden in adults with sickle cell disease predicts pain, depression, anxiety, health care utilization, and quality of life: The PiSCES project. *Psychosomatics, 52*(3), 272–279. doi:10.1016/j.psym.2011.01.010

Unal, S., Toros, F., Kutuk, M. O., & Uyaniker, M. G. (2011). Evaluation of the psychological problems in children with sickle cell anemia and their families. *Pediatric Hematology and Oncology, 28*(4), 321–328. doi:10.3109/08880018.2010.540735

Zempsky, W. T. (2009). Treatment of sickle cell pain: Fostering trust and justice. *JAMA, 302*, 2479–2480. doi:10.1001/jama.2009.1811

Zempsky, W. T. (2010). Evaluation and treatment of sickle cell pain in the emergency department: Paths to a better future. *Clinical Pediatric Emergency Medicine, 11*(4), 265–273. doi:10.1016/j.cpem.2010.09.002

Teresa Works, LCSW, ACSW, *is a clinical social worker and* **Sasia Jones, MPH,** *is a research assistant, New England Sickle Cell Institute, Carole and Ray Neag Comprehensive Cancer Center, University of Connecticut Health, Farmington.* **James Grady, PhD,** *is professor, Community Medicine and Health Care, University of Connecticut Health, Farmington.* **Biree Andemariam, MD,** *is assistant professor of medicine, Division of Hematology/Oncology, Carole and Ray Neag Comprehensive Cancer Center, and director of the New England Sickle Cell Institute, Farmington. Address correspondence to Biree Andemariam, New England Sickle Cell Institute, Carole and Ray Neag Comprehensive Cancer Center, University of Connecticut Health, 263 Farmington Avenue, Farmington, CT 06030; e-mail: andemariam@uchc.edu.*

Original manuscript received June 25, 2014
Final revision received December 22, 2014
Accepted February 12, 2015
Advance Access Publication December 13, 2015

Effectiveness of an Ongoing, Community-Based Breast Cancer Prevention Program for Korean American Women

Eun Koh, Ga-Young Choi, and Ji Young Cho

The study evaluates the effectiveness of an ongoing, community-based breast cancer prevention program offered by a local social services agency in the Washington, DC, metropolitan area. Korean American women who participated in this breast cancer prevention program were compared with those who did not participate in their knowledge, attitude, and screening behaviors. The study found that the intervention group was more knowledgeable on breast cancer and related services and reported more positive attitudes toward breast cancer screening services than the comparison group. The participants in the intervention group were also more likely to plan to receive a mammogram than those in the comparison group. However, significant differences were not observed in the two groups in their intention to receive a clinical breast examination. The study findings suggest that an ongoing, community-based breast cancer prevention program can be an effective method of addressing breast cancer prevention disparities observed among Korean American women.

KEY WORDS: *breast cancer; Korean American women; prevention program*

Racial and ethnic minorities are medically underserved populations in the United States, and the social work profession is committed to eliminating such racial and ethnic disparities in health care (National Association of Social Workers [NASW], n.d.). Breast cancer prevention is an area in which racial and ethnic health disparities are observed. In the current study, we focused on the experiences of Asian American women, particularly Korean American women in the Washington, DC, metropolitan area.

Asian American women have lower rates of breast cancer incidence and mortality compared with white, black, and Hispanic populations (Centers for Disease Control and Prevention [CDC], 2012). However, breast cancer is the most common cancer for Asian American women (Gomez et al., 2013), and its incidence rates have continued to increase over time. For example, between 2000 and 2009 the overall breast cancer incidence rate in the general population dropped, but the rate increased significantly, by 0.8 percent every year, for Asian and Pacific Islander women (CDC, 2012). This is partly due to Asian and Pacific Islander women having the lowest breast cancer screening rate in comparison with other racial and ethnic groups (CDC, 2012; Juon, Seo, & Kim, 2002; Office on Women's Health, 2010). Korean American women, particularly, are reported to be the least likely to receive breast cancer screening services among Asian groups (H. Y. Lee, Ju, Vang, & Lundquist, 2010).

Furthermore, Korean American women encounter additional challenges in obtaining breast cancer screening services. For example, fear of cancer and cancer treatment was common among Korean American women (S. Lee et al., 2013; Suh, 2006), as were feelings of embarrassment and shyness in discussing breast cancer–related issues (Han, Williams, & Harrison, 2000; Suh, 2006). Limited English proficiency (Choi et al., 2010; Juon, Choi, & Kim, 2000; S. Lee et al., 2013) and lack of health insurance (Kagawa-Singer & Pourat, 2000) are also identified barriers to breast cancer prevention services for this population. However, literature on breast cancer prevention programs for Korean American women, especially in the field of social work, is scarce (Suh, 2006). To fill in this gap, we investigated the effectiveness of a breast cancer screening program offered in a local community agency in three outcome areas: (1) participants' knowledge of breast cancer and its prevention, (2) participants' attitude toward breast cancer and its prevention, and (3) breast cancer screening behaviors.

LITERATURE REVIEW

Although limited, steady and continuing efforts have been made to implement and evaluate breast cancer prevention programs that specifically target Korean American women. In this section, we briefly discuss theoretical frameworks of the study, the health belief model (HBM), and cultural explanatory models (CEMs) and review prior studies that examined breast cancer prevention programs for Korean American women.

The HBM is one of the most common theories in breast cancer research (Yarbrough & Braden, 2001). The HBM hypothesizes that individuals will engage in breast cancer screening behaviors if they perceive that (a) they are vulnerable to breast cancer, (b) breast cancer is a serious illness, (c) screening behaviors are effective methods of preventing breast cancer, and (d) the benefits of breast cancer screening services exceed the barriers (for example, costs) of obtaining them (Champion & Skinner, 2008; Rosenstock, Strecher, & Becker, 1988). Many breast cancer prevention programs incorporate the HBM, teaching participants breast cancer screening methods, benefits of early screening, and symptoms of breast cancer (Han et al., 2000; Park, Chung, & Cochrane, 2013; Sadler, Ryujin, Ko, & Nguyen, 2001). For instance, Sadler et al. (2001) offered an educational prevention program incorporating the HBM to promote Korean American women's awareness of the significance of breast cancer screening behaviors; they reported positive outcomes in the participants' breast cancer screening behaviors.

Although the HBM is helpful in understanding women's breast cancer screening behaviors, it is limited in its ability to explain sociocultural determinants of health behaviors (Simon, 2006): It cannot describe how sociocultural contexts of the Korean American community would influence Korean American women's attitude toward breast cancer or screening behaviors, or their access to health care services (Rajaram & Rashidi, 1998). CEMs can complement the HBM, as they recognize the effects of socioeconomic factors such as limited English proficiency, cultural beliefs, financial resources, and repeated unpleasant experiences in medical systems in relation to Korean American women's breast cancer screening behaviors (Rajaram & Rashidi, 1998).

The characteristics of CEMs are observed in existing studies on breast cancer prevention services for Korean American communities (Juon, Choi, Klassen, & Roter, 2006; E. Lee et al., 2014; Maxwell, Jo, Crespi, Sudan, & Bastani, 2010; Moskowitz, Kazinets, Wong, & Tager, 2007; Sadler et al., 2001; Sadler et al., 2012). For example, in the study by Juon et al. (2006), the breast cancer prevention program consisted of a Korean-dubbed video on how to conduct breast self-examination; a photo novel in Korean; and small-group education on the prevalence, risk factors, early warning signs, and symptoms of breast and cervical cancers. The intervention also offered information on screening methods and guidelines as well as free or low-cost mammogram screening services available in the community. At the end of the study period, participants' intention to get a mammogram was approximately three times higher for the intervention group than for the control group, suggesting the effectiveness of the culturally tailored program.

In the current study, we examined the impact of a community-based breast cancer prevention program for Korean American women. The program is based on the theoretical frameworks of the HBM and CEMs, and it has been offered by a local community agency for Korean Americans in the Washington, DC, metropolitan area that has an established relationship with this population. Given the limited literature on breast cancer prevention programs for Korean American women, with this study, we attempt to increase knowledge in this area. Furthermore, very few studies, if any, have investigated an ongoing breast cancer prevention program offered by a community social services agency. In the majority of prior studies that involved Korean American women, one-time programs were offered (Juon et al., 2006; E. Lee et al., 2014; Maxwell et al., 2010; Sadler et al., 2001). It is thus unknown whether such programs will lead to similar results when provided as ongoing services by a local community agency. The findings of the study will offer knowledge and insight into whether ongoing, community-based breast cancer prevention programs can result in the same level of effectiveness as observed in one-time prevention programs.

The current study is also distinctive in that the prevention program in the study provides actual breast cancer screening services, whereas prior studies primarily focused on educational activities in their breast cancer prevention efforts (Juon et al., 2006; E. Lee et al., 2014; Sadler et al., 2012). A mammogram was offered as part of the program in Moskowitz et al.'s (2007) study, but the main focus of the study was still the effectiveness of community health education. In addition, although free or low-cost mammogram services were the main prevention program in Kim and Sarna's (2004) study, it was offered as a one-time service. Addressing these gaps in the existing literature, we investigated the effects of a community-based breast cancer prevention program for Korean American women on their knowledge, attitude, and screening behaviors in relation to breast cancer and its prevention.

METHOD
Breast Cancer Prevention Program

The breast cancer prevention program in this study was first offered by the aforementioned local community agency in 2009. The program has two components. One is targeted toward broader Korean communities in the area, providing information on breast cancer and its prevention and educating residents about the importance of screening behaviors. Here, the agency attempts to reach as many Korean American men and women as it can, using DVDs and conducting educational workshops at local Korean American religious or community organizations. The DVDs and workshops were mainly presented in Korean. The other component of the program involves providing actual breast cancer screening services (that is, clinical breast examination [CBE], mammogram, or both) for Korean American women through a health fair at no cost to the participants, which is the focus of the current study. These screening services were developed and implemented while keeping in mind the challenges many Korean American women experience in accessing and using breast cancer screening services, which are largely due to their limited English proficiency (Choi et al., 2010; Juon et al., 2000; S. Lee et al., 2013; Sadler et al., 2012) and lack of health insurance (Kagawa-Singer & Pourat, 2000).

As of June 2012, the program was offered to a total of 985 Korean Americans, excluding the people who had obtained the educational DVDs. This figure includes Korean American women who received more than one service (that is, of CBE, mammogram, and workshops) or who received the same service more than once. A steady increase has been observed in the number of service recipients each year, going from 86 people in 2009 to 252 in 2011. Specifically, 65 and 86 Korean American women received a CBE and a mammogram, respectively, in 2011, and 101 Korean Americans attended the educational workshops in the same year.

Sample Selection and Data Collection Procedures

In the study, Korean American women who received breast cancer screening services were compared with those who did not in three outcome areas: (1) knowledge of breast cancer and prevention services, (2) attitude regarding breast cancer and prevention services, and (3) intention to receive breast cancer screening services. Out of 404 Korean American women who received the screening services (that is, CBE, mammogram, or both) from the agency, contact information was available for 289 women. For the intervention group, 100 women were randomly selected out of these 289 service recipients. A convenient and snowball sampling method was used to select 111 Korean American women for the comparison group who reportedly did not receive the breast cancer screening services from the agency. The participants were mainly recruited from Korean American religious organizations and with the use of the agency staff's personal and professional network. As a result, a total of 211 Korean American women participated in the study. Telephone or in-person surveys using a structured questionnaire were conducted with the selected participants between May 2012 and August 2012.

Measurements

A structured questionnaire was developed using existing measurement tools. To measure the participants' knowledge on breast cancer and screening services, we adopted a total of 10 items (for example, "Mammogram is able to detect small lesions which cannot be felt by self-examination") from a study by Hur et al. (2009), who had created these items on the basis of prior studies (C. Y. Lee, Kim, Ko, & Ham, 2003; Skinner, Arfken, & Sykes, 1998). The participants' responses were coded as correct or incorrect, with 1 assigned for the correct ones. The possible scores ranged from 0 to 10, with higher scores indicating more knowledge. An additional question, which was adopted from the *ka lei mana'olana* project survey (Ka'opua, Park, Ward, & Braun, 2011), examined the participants' knowledge on the symptoms of breast cancer by asking participants to mark the correct symptoms out of five response options.

To measure the participants' attitudes toward breast cancer screening services, one item was adopted from the *ka lei mana'olana* project survey (Ka'opua et al., 2011) and two items were created on the basis of a study by Fallowfield, Rodway, and Baum (1990) (for example, "My health is too good at present even to consider thinking that I might get breast cancer"). The participants were asked to indicate on four-point Likert-type scales the extent to which they would agree with a given statement. Higher scores implied the participants were more likely to recognize the significance of or the need for breast cancer screening services, with a possible maximum score of 12.

To measure their intention to receive breast cancer screening services, we asked the participants whether they were planning to receive a CBE and a mammogram in the given year. When the participants indicated that they planned to receive screening services or responded that they had already obtained the services for the given year, they were considered to have the intention to obtain the screening services.

In addition to the items on the study outcomes, the questionnaire inquired about the participants' demographic information, such as age, marital status, living arrangement, level of income, educational attainment, health insurance, and length of stay in the United States.

DATA ANALYTIC METHODS

We initially compared the two groups using t tests and simple chi-square tests. The t tests were conducted for the outcomes of knowledge (regarding breast cancer and screening services) and attitudes, and the chi-square tests were used for the outcomes of additional knowledge (on symptoms of breast cancer) and intention to receive screening services. Multiple regression and logistic regression analyses were completed to further examine the effect of the program when controlling for the influence of the other variables, especially considering the significant differences observed between the two groups. In addition to the independent variable of the study (that is, intervention versus comparison groups), the following controlling variables were included in the model on the basis of the findings of prior literature and subject to data availability: the participants' age, level of income, educational attainment, insurance coverage, length of stay in the United States, and prior receipt of breast cancer screening services (Choi et al., 2010; Glenn, Chawla, Surani, & Bastani, 2009; Juon et al., 2006; Kagawa-Singer & Pourat, 2000; E. Lee et al., 2014). Because the literature identifies family members' encouragement as one of the factors promoting Korean women's use of breast cancer screening services (Han et al., 2000), the participants' marital status and living arrangement were also included as controlling variables.

FINDINGS
Sample Description

The agency only offers the breast cancer screening services to Korean American women with low socioeconomic status, and this led to significant differences between the intervention and the comparison groups in all demographic variables except for age and length of time they had lived in the United States (see Table 1). Although the mean age was not statistically significantly different between the two groups ($p = .973$), the participants in the comparison group had a wider range of ages: The ages ranged from 40 to 70 years for the intervention group, whereas the range was from 29 to 87 years for the comparison group. The participants from the intervention group were more likely than those in the comparison group to be married at the time of the survey (92.0 percent versus 70.3 percent, respectively; $p < .001$). The intervention group had a significantly lower level of income and educational attainment, and the proportion of the participants with some type of health insurance was significantly lower for them. For instance, the majority of the intervention group participants did not have any type of health insurance, but approximately half of the comparison group participants reported having some type of health insurance ($p < .001$). Last, the two groups were significantly different in their previous experience of breast cancer screening services: More participants from the intervention group reported having received a mammogram at some point, but the percentage of participants who ever received a CBE was higher for the comparison group. It should be noted that only the participants 40 years of age or older were included in the comparison of the two groups in their prior receipt of a mammogram, considering that a mammogram is recommended for this age group (National Cancer Institute, 2014).

Knowledge, Attitude, and Behavior

The two groups were first compared on their knowledge of breast cancer and related services (see Table 2). The participants in the intervention group were found to be significantly more knowledgeable on breast

Table 1: Sample Characteristics and Frequency

Characteristic	Intervention Group (n = 100) M (SD)	Intervention Group n (%)	Comparison Group (n = 111) M (SD)	Comparison Group n (%)
Age (in years)[a]	53.9 (7.6)		53.8 (13.2)	
Marital status				
Single		0* (0.0)		7 (6.3)
Married		92*** (92.0)		78 (70.3)
Separated, divorced, or widowed		8* (8.0)		21 (18.9)
No response provided		0 (0.0)		5 (4.5)
Living arrangement				
Live alone		4*** (4.0)		22 (19.8)
Live only with spouse		28 (28.0)		27 (24.3)
Live with spouse and other family members		62* (62.0)		50 (45.0)
Other living arrangements		6 (6.0)		10 (9.0)
No response provided		0 (0.0)		2 (1.8)
Yearly household income				
Less than $15,000		22 (22.0)		19 (17.1)
$15,000 to $24,999		27** (27.0)		14 (12.6)
$25,000 to $49,999		46* (46.0)		33 (29.7)
More than $50,000		4*** (4.0)		31 (27.9)
No response provided		1*** (1.0)		14 (12.6)
Educational attainment				
Less than high school		13 (13.0)		14 (12.6)
High school or equivalent (GED)		42*** (42.0)		22 (19.8)
Business or technical training or associate degree		14 (14.0)		15 (13.5)
Bachelor's degree		28 (28.0)		37 (33.3)
Graduate school or equivalent		2** (2.0)		15 (13.5)
No response provided		1* (1.0)		8 (7.2)
Insurance				
Yes		9*** (9.0)		55 (49.5)
No		91*** (91.0)		42 (37.8)
No response provided		0*** (0.0)		14 (12.6)
Years in the United States	15.1 (8.7)		17.4 (11.4)	
Ever received a clinical breast examination				
Yes		22*** (22.0)		79 (71.2)
No		76*** (76.0)		29 (26.1)
No response provided		2 (2.0)		3 (2.7)
Ever received a mammogram[b]				
Yes		89* (89.0)		62 (68.1)
No		11* (11.0)		22 (24.2)
No response provided		0**		7 (7.7)

[a]From the comparison group, five participants did not report their age.
[b]From the comparison group, 20 participants were younger than 40 years.
*$p < .05$. **$p < .01$. ***$p < .001$.

cancer–related issues than were those in the comparison group: The mean score for the intervention group was 7.4, whereas it was 6.4 for the comparison group ($p < .001$). In addition, the proportion of the participants who marked all three correct symptoms out of five response options was larger for the intervention group than for the comparison group (51.0 percent versus 36.0 percent; $p < .05$). The two groups also differed in their attitudes on breast cancer screening services: The participants in the intervention group scored higher on their attitude than did those in the comparison group: The average scores were 9.8 and 8.1, respectively, for the two groups ($p < .001$).

The intention to receive mammogram services was significantly different between the two groups, but the intention to obtain a CBE was not (see Table 2). More than two-thirds of the intervention group had already received or were planning to receive mammogram services for the given year, whereas the comparable percentage was only 57.5

percent for the comparison group ($p < .01$). Again, the analysis excluded 20 participants in the comparison group who were younger than 40 years.

The findings of multiple regression and logistic regression analyses were consistent with the results of the bivariate analyses (see Table 3). The intervention group was more knowledgeable on breast cancer and related services and was more likely to recognize the significance of and need for breast cancer screening services than were those in the comparison group: Such differences held even after the addition of the controlling variables. However, inclusion of the controlling variables lowered the significance level to .05 for the first knowledge outcome and resulted in no significant differences between the two groups for the second knowledge outcome ($p = .103$). Similarly, more participants from the intervention group reported their intention to receive a mammogram. Such significant difference between the two groups persisted but decreased after the addition of the controlling variables. The two groups were similar in the participants' intention to obtain a CBE.

Table 2: Bivariate Analyses on Participants' Knowledge, Attitude, and Behavior

Variable	Intervention Group ($n = 100$)		Comparison Group ($n = 111$)		Test Statistics
	M (SD)	n (%)	M (SD)	n (%)	
Knowledge score[a]	7.4 (1.6)		6.4 (2.1)		$t(208, 209) = 3.6***$
Identified all three correct symptoms		51.0		36.0	$\chi^2(1) = 4.8*$
Attitude score	9.8 (1.4)		8.1 (1.9)		$t(208, 209) = 7.5***$
Intend to receive a clinical breast examination[b]					
Yes		53.0		58.9	$\chi^2(1) = 0.7$
No		47.0		41.1	
Intend to receive a mammogram[b,c]					
Yes		78.0		57.5	$\chi^2(1) = 9.1**$
No		22.0		42.5	

[a]From the comparison group, one participant did not respond.
[b]From the comparison group, four participants did not respond.
[c]From the comparison group, 20 participants were younger than 40 years.
*$p < .05$. **$p < .01$. ***$p < .001$.

Table 3: Regression Analyses on Participants' Knowledge, Attitude, and Behavior

Outcome	Group Membership (Intervention versus Comparison Group)	
	B	SE
Knowledge on breast cancer and related services		
Without controlling variables	0.967****	0.273
With controlling variables added into the model	0.778*	0.372
Knowledge on breast cancer symptoms		
Without controlling variables	0.990**	0.330
With controlling variables added into the model	0.750	0.460
Attitude on breast cancer screening services		
Without controlling variables	1.736***	0.259
With controlling variables added into the model	1.765***	0.372
Intention to receive a clinical breast exam		
Without controlling variables	−0.199	0.310
With controlling variables added into the model	0.208	0.444
Intention to receive a mammogram		
Without controlling variables	1.099**	0.339
With controlling variables added into the model	1.010*	0.481

Note: Considering the space limitation and the main purpose of the study, the statistics for the controlling variables are not reported. Instead, the controlling variables whose effect was reported to be significant are listed: (1) level of education ($p < .1$) and health insurance coverage ($p < .1$) for the first outcome of knowledge, (2) length of stay in the United States ($p < .1$) for the second outcome of knowledge, (3) none for the outcome of attitude, (4) prior receipt of a clinical breast exam (CBE) ($p < .1$) for the outcome of intention to receive a CBE, and (5) age ($p < .1$) and prior receipt of a mammogram ($p < .01$) for the outcome of intention to receive a mammogram.
*$p < .05$. **$p < .01$. ***$p < .001$.

DISCUSSION

This study demonstrated that an ongoing community-based breast cancer prevention program can be an effective method in addressing the disparity in breast cancer prevention observed for Korean American women. In this study, the program resulted in the similar efficacy in the participants' knowledge, attitude, and behaviors as observed for short-term educational programs in the existing literature. Specifically, the study found that the intervention group was more knowledgeable on breast cancer screening services and reported more positive attitudes toward breast cancer screening services than the comparison group did. The participants in the intervention group were also more likely than those in the comparison group to plan to receive a mammogram. Such effects remained significant even after the addition of the controlling variables, including the prior receipt of a mammogram.

It is plausible, based on the HBM (E. Lee et al., 2014), that these effects were due to the participants' interaction with medical professionals via the program, thereby increasing their knowledge of breast cancer and its prevention, their positive attitude toward breast cancer screening services, and their future intention to receive mammogram services. The findings on the participants' intention to receive a CBE were somewhat unexpected, even though a few studies reported no significant effectiveness of the prevention programs on this outcome (Moskowitz et al., 2007; Park et al., 2013). However, it is notable that the two groups were similar in this outcome, even though a significantly larger number of the participants in the comparison group previously received a CBE.

The positive outcomes of the ongoing, community-based breast cancer prevention program in the current study suggest the need for those in the social work profession to take more active roles in developing, implementing, and evaluating community-based breast cancer prevention programs. Through empowerment, social workers can engage Korean American communities in breast cancer prevention efforts. For example, social workers can advocate for the needs of the community to medical professionals, provide emotional support, and work with community members to establish accessible breast cancer prevention services. The scarce literature on breast cancer prevention programs for Korean American women, especially from the field of social work, implies the profession's limited engagement and services for this underserved, understudied population. Given the profession's commitment to health parity, especially for underserved populations, more effort should be made to expand prevention programs within Korean American communities.

Furthermore, the findings on the study sample as well as the program effectiveness confirm the need for culturally tailored breast cancer prevention programs for the Korean American population, as suggested by CEMs (Rajaram & Rashidi, 1998). As the intervention was mainly offered in Korean, it may be that the participants felt more comfortable receiving a mammogram and communicating with the medical staff regarding breast cancer compared with those who did not take part in the program. In the study, it was also noted that the majority of the participants in the intervention group had no health insurance, and approximately half of the comparison group reported that they had some type of health insurance. This is consistent with prior literature that reports low rates of health insurance coverage for Korean Americans (Shin, Song, Kim, & Probst, 2005), which is a significant barrier to their receipt of preventive medical services, including breast cancer screening (Kagawa-Singer & Pourat, 2000). These socioeconomic circumstances of Korean American women should be considered when planning the development and delivery of prevention programs. Because the data collection of the study was completed before implementation of the Patient Protection and Affordable Care Act in 2010 (P.L. 111-148), it will be worthwhile to investigate whether the act has increased the insurance coverage for Korean American women and whether it has led to changes in their breast cancer screening behaviors.

Despite the promising and notable findings of the current study, they should be interpreted with caution considering the limited rigor of the study design. The intervention and comparison groups were not comparable, and it is unknown to what extent the observed outcomes are attributable to such group differences. Furthermore, because the study focused on a community-based breast cancer prevention program that is ongoing, it is difficult to understand what components of the program account for the observed outcomes. That is, it is unclear whether the findings are due to the actual provision of the services or to the information the participants may have received during the receipt of the services. In addition, because of the cross-sectional nature of the study, the influence of the intervention on actual breast cancer screening behaviors was not investigated.

However, the current study is significant in that it shows the potential of a community-based breast cancer prevention program that is tailored to a specific ethnic group and its social, cultural, and economic characteristics. This, in turn, requires the cultural competence of social workers in multifaceted manners, including cross-cultural knowledge and skills, culturally competent service delivery, and language diversity (NASW, 2001), throughout all phases of program development, implementation, and evaluation. These efforts have the potential to lead to the elimination of breast health disparities for this population. HSW

REFERENCES

Centers for Disease Control and Prevention. (2012). *Breast cancer statistics*. Retrieved from http://www.cdc.gov/cancer/breast/statistics/index.htm

Champion, V. L., & Skinner, C. S. (2008). The health belief model. In K. Glanz, B. K. Rimer, & K. Viswanath (Eds.), *Health behavior and health education: Theory, research, and practice* (4th ed., pp. 45–66). San Francisco: Jossey-Bass.

Choi, K. S., Lee, S., Park, E.-C., Kwak, M.-S., Spring, B. J., & Juon, H.-S. (2010). Comparison of breast cancer screening rates between Korean women in America versus Korea. *Journal of Women's Health, 19*, 1089–1096.

Fallowfield, L. J., Rodway, A., & Baum, M. (1990). What are the psychological factors influencing attendance, non-attendance and re-attendance at a breast screening center? *Journal of the Royal Society of Medicine, 83*, 547–551.

Glenn, B. A., Chawla, N., Surani, Z., & Bastani, R. (2009). Rates and sociodemographic correlates of cancer screening among South Asians. *Journal of Community Health, 34*, 113–121.

Gomez, S. L., Noone, A. M., Lichtensztajn, D. Y., Scoppa, S., Gibson, J. T., Liu, L., et al. (2013). Cancer incidence trends among Asian American populations in the United States, 1990–2008. *Journal of the National Cancer Institute, 105*, 1096–1110.

Han, Y., Williams, R. D., & Harrison, R. A. (2000). Breast cancer screening knowledge, attitudes, and practice among Korean American women. *Oncology Nursing Forum, 27*, 1585–1591.

Hur, H. K., Park, S. M., Kim, C. H., Park, J. K., Koh, S. B., & Kim, G. Y. (2009). Development of an integrated breast health program for prevention of breast cancer among middle-aged women. *Korean Journal of Women Health Nursing, 15*, 54–63.

Juon, H. S., Choi, Y., & Kim, M. T. (2000). Cancer screening behaviors among Korean American women. *Cancer Detection and Prevention, 24*, 589–601.

Juon, H. S., Choi, S., Klassen, A., & Roter, D. (2006). Impact of breast cancer screening intervention on Korean-American women in Maryland. *Cancer Detection and Prevention, 30*, 297–305.

Juon, H. S., Seo, Y., & Kim, M. T. (2002). Breast and cervical cancer screening among Korean American elderly women. *European Journal of Oncology Nursing, 6*, 228–235.

Kagawa-Singer, M., & Pourat, N. (2000). Asian American and Pacific Islander breast and cervical carcinoma screening rates and Healthy People 2000 objectives. *Cancer, 89*, 696–705.

Ka'opua, L. S. I., Park, S. H., Ward, M. E., & Braun, K. L. (2011). Testing the feasibility of a culturally tailored breast cancer screening intervention with native Hawaiian women in rural churches. *Health & Social Work, 36*, 55–65.

Kim, Y. H., & Sarna, L. (2004). An intervention to increase mammography use by Korean American women. *Oncology Nursing Forum, 31*, 105–110.

Lee, C. Y., Kim, H. S., Ko, S., & Ham, O. K. (2003). Evaluation of a community-based program for breast self-examination offered by the community health nurse practitioners in Korea. *Journal of Korean Academy of Nursing, 33*, 1119–1126.

Lee, E., Menon, U., Nandy, K., Szalacha, L., Kviz, F., Cho, Y., et al. (2014). The effect of a couples intervention to increase breast cancer screening among Korean Americans. *Oncology Nursing Forum, 41*, E185–E193. doi:10.1188/14.0NF.E185-E193

Lee, H. Y., Ju, E., Vang, P., & Lundquist, M. (2010). Breast and cervical cancer screening among Asian American women and Latinas: Does race/ethnicity matter? *Journal of Women's Health, 19*, 1877–1884.

Lee, S., Chen, L., Ma, G. X., Fang, C. Y., Oh, Y., & Scully, L. (2013). Challenges and needs of Chinese and Korean American breast cancer survivors: In-depth interviews. *North American Journal of Medicine and Science, 6*, 1–8.

Maxwell, A. E., Jo, A. M., Crespi, C. M., Sudan, M., & Bastani, R. (2010). Peer navigation improves diagnostic follow-up after breast cancer screening among Korean American women: Results of a randomized trial. *Cancer Causes Control, 21*, 1931–1940.

Moskowitz, J. M., Kazinets, G., Wong, J. M., & Tager, I. B. (2007). "Health is strength": A community health education program to improve breast and cervical cancer screening among Korean American Women in Alameda County, California. *Cancer Detection and Prevention, 31*, 173–183.

National Association of Social Workers. (2001). *NASW standards for cultural competence in social work practice*. Retrieved from http://www.socialworkers.org/practice/standards/NASWCulturalStandards.pdf

National Association of Social Workers. (n.d.). *Social work & health care disparities*. Retrieved from http://www.socialworkers.org/advocacy/briefing/HealthCareDisparitiesBriefingPaper.pdf

National Cancer Institute. (2014). *Mammograms*. Retrieved from http://www.cancer.gov/cancertopics/factsheet/detection/mammograms

Office on Women's Health. (2010). *Minority women's health: Breast cancer*. Retrieved from http://womenshealth.gov/minority-health/asian-americans/breast-cancer.html

Park, S., Chung, C., & Cochrane, B. B. (2013). Effects of tailored message education about breast cancer risk appraisal for obese Korean women. *Oncology Nursing Forum, 40*, E382–E392.

Rajaram, S. S., & Rashidi, A. (1998). Minority women and breast cancer screening: The role of cultural explanatory models. *Preventive Medicine, 27*, 757–764.

Rosenstock, I. M., Strecher, V. J., & Becker, M. H. (1988). Social learning theory and the health belief model. *Health Education Quarterly, 15*, 175–183.

Sadler, G. R., Beerman, P. R., Lee, K., Hung, J., Nguyen, H., Cho, J., & Huang, W. (2012). Promoting breast cancer screening among Asian American women:

The Asian grocery store-based cancer education program. *Journal of Cancer Education, 27,* 612–617.

Sadler, G. R., Ryujin, L. T., Ko, C. M., & Nguyen, E. (2001). Korean women: Breast cancer knowledge, attitudes and behaviors. *BMC Public Health, 1,* Article 7. doi:10.1186/1471-2458-1-7

Shin, H., Song, H., Kim, J., & Probst, J. C. (2005). Insurance, acculturation, and health service utilization among Korean-Americans. *Journal of Immigrant Health, 7,* 65–74.

Simon, C. E. (2006). Breast cancer screening: Cultural beliefs and diverse populations. *Health & Social Work, 31,* 36–43.

Skinner, C. S., Arfken, C. L., & Kykes, R. K. (1998). Knowledge, perceptions, and mammography stage of adoption among older urban women. *American Journal of Preventive Medicine, 14,* 54–63.

Suh, E. E. (2006). Korean immigrant women's meaning of breast, breast cancer, and breast cancer screening. *Journal of Korean Academy of Nursing, 36,* 604–611.

Yarbrough, S. S., & Braden, C. J. (2001). Utility of health belief model as a guide for explaining or predicting breast cancer screening behaviours. *Journal of Advanced Nursing, 33,* 677–688.

***

Eun Koh, PhD, *is assistant professor, National Catholic School of Social Service, Catholic University of America, Shahan Hall 111, 620 Michigan Avenue, NE, Washington, DC 20064; e-mail: koh@cua.edu.* **Ga-Young Choi, PhD,** *is assistant professor, Department of Social Work, College of Social and Behavioral Sciences, University of Northern Iowa, Cedar Falls.* **Ji Young Cho, PhD,** *is executive director, Korean Community Service Center of Greater Washington, Annandale, VA.*

Original manuscript received October 1, 2014
Final revision received February 5, 2015
Accepted February 18, 2015
Advance Access Publication December 16, 2015

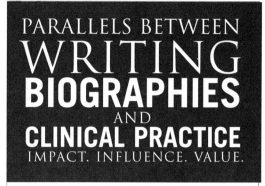

ESTHER URDANG

Parallels between Writing Biographies and Clinical Practice: Impact. Influence. Value offers clinicians an in-depth understanding of the commonalities between the psychological and intellectual processes involved in writing biographical works and those involved in clinical practice. Although these processes often take place beneath the surface, both biographers and clinicians are subjectively involved in all aspects of their work, such as the biases of their theoretical positions and selection and evaluation of evidence.

Parallels between Writing Biographies and Clinical Practice is a resource intended for students, teachers, and practitioners in social work, and those in the human services and medical professions. It is also intended for a general audience, to heighten critical understanding and enjoyment in the reading of biographies.

ISBN: 978-0-87101-450-4. 2014.
Item #4504. 304 pages. $36.99.
1-800-227-3590 • www.naswpress.org

NASW PRESS

CODE APWB14

PRACTICE FORUM

Using mHealth in Social Work Practice with Low-Income Hispanic Patients

Joyce Y. Lee and Sri Harathi

The Hispanic population is the fastest growing minority group in the United States. According to the U.S. Census Bureau (2006), by the year 2050 it is estimated that nearly one-quarter of the country's population, or 102.6 million, will be of Hispanic origin. However, this population falls behind other ethnic and racial groups in terms of median years of education and annual household income (Gutiérrez, Yeakley, & Ortega, 2000). In addition to poor socioeconomic status, Hispanic people—especially recent immigrants—face issues related to cultural and language barriers that hinder them from seeking and accessing basic health care services (Escarce & Kapur, 2006). As a result, the predominantly low-income Hispanic population is at risk of various health maladies, including diabetes, hypertension, and major depression, without proper access to timely and quality health care provision (Centers for Disease Control and Prevention, 2014; Padilla, Ruiz, & Alvarez, 1989; Sieverdes et al., 2013).

In addition, the Hispanic population is one of the country's most disproportionately uninsured groups. During the first year of enrollment, only 2.6 million out of 10.2 million uninsured Hispanic people eligible for health care coverage through the 2010 Patient Protection and Affordable Care Act (ACA) (P.L. 111-148) signed up for health plans (U.S. Department of Health and Human Services, 2012). Health insurance reduces out-of-pocket costs and has been shown to be the single most important predictor of health care utilization (Escarce & Kapur, 2006). Without health insurance, many Hispanic people forgo not only care even when they need it, but also the opportunity to establish a usual source of care. Having a usual source of care provides a locus of entry into the complex health care delivery system and serves as the link to more specialized types of care (Lewin-Epstein, 1991). However, minority groups such as low-income Hispanic people are less likely to seek specialized health care services and instead rely on public clinics or informal support systems (Furman et al., 2009).

Given these barriers, social work practitioners working closely with Hispanic patients are urged to apply innovative practice methods to help reduce the health care gap prevalent among this population. In particular, Norris and Alegria (2005) have argued that social workers should develop and implement health care services that allow for more flexible hours, elicit feedback from clients, and are more culturally sensitive. In response, researchers have suggested using mobile technology to help fill these service gaps and meet the specific health needs of Hispanic patients (Aguilera & Muñoz, 2011). Meanwhile, it is also important to note the rapidly increasing number of cell phone owners among this population because such a pattern implies mobile technology's potential to effectively deliver appropriate health-related services. With its availability and affordability, mobile technology is continuously identified as a vital tool that supports health assessment, treatment, and client engagement (Seko, Kidd, Wiljer, & McKenzie, 2014). Building on such evidence from previous studies, this article explores most recent practice interventions and action research using mobile technology to address critical health needs among low-income Hispanic patients. Furthermore, it draws important implications for social workers striving to create a more equitable health care system for this population by illuminating the advantages and challenges of using mobile technology in social work practice in health settings.

CELL PHONE OWNERSHIP AMONG THE HISPANIC POPULATION

As of 2014, Hispanic adults scored the highest (92 percent) among those who own cell phones (compared with 90 percent white and 90 percent African American) (Pew Research Center, 2014). Although younger and more educated Hispanic adults are more likely to report their cell phone ownerships,

56 percent Hispanic adults 65 and older, 77 percent with less than a high school diploma, and 83 percent with annual family incomes below $30,000 also say that they own at least one cell phone (Lopez, Gonzalez-Barrera, & Patten, 2013). Given the prevalence of cell phones in Hispanic communities across age, educational level, and annual income, mobile technology is considered to be promising for improving access to health care for this group, especially Hispanic patients in resource-limited settings. Mobile technology used in health settings is often referred to as mHealth, which implies the use of mobile communication—such as applications and text messaging—to promote an individual's health by supporting key health care practices (for example, health data collection, delivery of health care information, or patient self-observation) (World Health Organization, 2011).

MOBILE DIABETIC TREATMENT

To examine the preliminary effectiveness of mHealth intervention on low-income and bilingual Hispanic patients with poorly controlled diabetes, Arora, Peters, Agy, and Menchine (2012) conducted a proof-of-concept trial using the Trial to Examine Text-Based mHealth for Emergency Department Patients with Diabetes (abbreviated as TExT-MED) program, a text message–based intervention designed specifically for low-income diabetic patients. The researchers used a sample of 23 diabetic patients (70 percent Hispanic). Patients received three text messages a day for three weeks in English and Spanish on educational information about diabetes, healthy goal setting, and medication reminders. The study results showed that in the week before TExT-MED, 56.5 percent reported eating fruits or vegetables daily versus 83 percent after the intervention, 43.5 percent reported exercising before versus 74 percent after, and 74 percent reported performing foot checks before versus 85 percent after. Self-efficacy and medication adherence scores also improved. Ninety percent of diabetic patients expressed their desire to continue the text message–based mHealth program.

HYPERTENSION TREATMENT

Similarly, Sieverdes and colleagues (2013) performed a proof-of-concept randomized control trial that examined the initial effectiveness of the Smartphone Medication Adherence Stops Hypertension (SMASH) intervention on 10 Hispanic patients with uncontrolled *essential hypertension*, a rise in blood pressure of unknown cause that also increases risks for cerebral, cardiac, and renal events (Messerli, Williams, Ritz, 2007). For a three-month period, cell phone–connected medication trays provided reminders for patients to take their medications while smartphone messages reminded patients to take at-home blood pressures. Health providers received bimonthly feedback and sent subsequent motivational and reinforcement text and audio messages to the patients. Results showed high provider and patient acceptability through high study recruitment (86 percent), high retention (100 percent), and good to excellent adherence to the intervention (average 97 percent adherence to medication regimen across trial, 83 percent adherence to a three-day blood pressure protocol, and 89 percent adherence to total blood pressure readings), suggesting that the SMASH intervention serves as a potentially effective tool assisting Hispanic patients in managing hypertension.

DEPRESSION TREATMENT

With respect to major depression among the Hispanic population, Aguilera and Munõz (2011) used automated text messages as an adjunct to group cognitive–behavioral therapy among low-income patients with depression. Twelve patients (five English speakers, seven Spanish speakers) in a public sector clinic received daily text messages in English or Spanish that asked questions about the total numbers of positive and negative thoughts, interpersonal contacts, and physical activities (for example, "How many positive thoughts have you noticed today?" "How many positive social interactions have you had today? "How many things have you done to improve your health today?"). After running the text messaging adjunct for two months, the study results showed a participant response rate of 65 percent with reports suggesting increased therapeutic alliances. In particular, Spanish-speaking patients reported that receiving messages made them feel closer to their therapists and encouraged them to attend group sessions. Overall, study results indicated that low-income Hispanic patients receiving psychotherapy in a community-based mental health care setting are responsive to and like using text messages as part of their treatment for depression (Aguilera & Munõz, 2011).

ADVANTAGES AND LIMITATIONS

For social work practitioners serving low-income Hispanic patients and striving to create a more equitable health care system on behalf of this population, it is important to note the key advantages of mHealth in improving access to health care. In addition to user friendliness, cost effectiveness, and flexibility, mHealth provides the added advantage of anonymity (Seko et al., 2014)—a potentially critical element for Hispanic patients who may be facing issues of immigration, language barriers, and sociocultural stigma attached to seeking certain health care services (for example, HIV/AIDS, depression). Because mobile platforms are usually visible only to the user, Hispanic patients wishing to seek health treatment while simultaneously protecting their identities may be more likely to use mHealth rather than traditional interventions. Most important, mHealth has been known to help strengthen the therapeutic alliance (Morris & Aguilera, 2012), or the professional helping relationship, which is one of the fundamental tenets of social work practice. Social workers are encouraged to incorporate mHealth interventions in their practice to strengthen helping relationships with Hispanic patients and better assist the navigation of and access to necessary health care services.

At the same time, social workers should also note two major mHealth limitations: (1) the issue of privacy concerning patients' digital health information and (2) paucity of evidence-based research (Shore et al., 2014). Because mHealth allows for continual and broad data collection as well as information sharing with multiple parties in a patient's network, it is imperative that social workers take extra precaution to ensure client confidentiality, especially for undocumented Hispanic patients whose immigration statuses often hinder them from seeking basic health treatment. In addition, there is a general lack of evidence-based research that supports the long-term effectiveness of mHealth in social work practice with socioeconomically disadvantaged and ethnic minority clients. Although this article highlighted recent practice interventions that are promising for improving the health care disparity for Hispanic patients, more randomized controlled longitudinal studies using larger samples need to be conducted. Taken together, social workers are urged to keep these mHealth limitations, as well as key benefits, in mind as they judiciously use mobile technology to assist their everyday practice with low-income Hispanic patients. **HSW**

REFERENCES

Aguilera, A., & Muñoz, R. F. (2011). Text messaging as an adjunct to CBT in low-income populations: A usability and feasability pilot study. *Professional Psychology: Research and Practice, 42*, 472–478.

Arora, S., Peters, A. L., Agy, D., & Menchine, M. (2012). A mobile health intervention for inner city patients with poorly controlled diabetes: Proof-of-concept of the TExT-MED program. *Diabetes Technology & Therapeutics, 14*, 492–497.

Centers for Disease Control and Prevention. (2014). *Minority health: Hispanic or Latino populations.* Retrieved from http://www.cdc.gov/minorityhealth/populations/REMP/hispanic.html#Gov

Escarce, J. J., & Kapur, K. (2006). Access to and quality of health care. In M. Tienda & F. Mitchell (Eds.), *Hispanics and the Future of America* (pp. 410–446). Washington, DC: National Academies Press.

Furman, R., Negi, N. J., Iwamoto, D. K., Rowan, D., Shukraft, A., & Gragg, J. (2009). Social work practice with Latinos: Key issues for social workers. *Social Work, 54*, 167–174.

Gutiérrez, L., Yeakley, A., & Ortega, R. (2000). Educating students for social work with Latinos: Issues for the new millennium. *Journal of Social Work Education, 36*, 541–557.

Lewin-Epstein, N. (1991). Determinants of regular source of health care in black, Mexican, Puerto Rican, and non-Hispanic white populations. *Medical Care, 29*, 543–557.

Lopez, M. H., Gonzalez-Barrera, A., & Patten, E. (2013). *Closing the digital divide: Latinos and technology adoption: III. Cellphone use.* Retrieved from http://www.pewhispanic.org/2013/03/07/iii-cellphone-use/

Messerli, F. H., Williams, B., & Ritz, E. (2007). Essential hypertension. *Lancet, 370*(9587), 591–603.

Morris, M. E., & Aguilera, A. (2012). Mobile, social, and wearable computing and the evolution of psychological practice. *Professional Psychology: Research and Practice, 43*, 622–626.

Norris, F., & Alegria, M. (2005). Mental health care for ethnic minority individuals and communities in the aftermath of disaster and mass violence. *CNS Spectrums, 10*, 132–140.

Padilla, A. M., Ruiz, R. A., & Alvarez, R. (1989). Community mental health services for the Spanish speaking/surname populations. In D. R. Atkinson, G. Morten, & D. W. Sue (Eds.), *Counseling American minorities: A cross-cultural perspective* (3rd ed., pp. 167–198). Dubuque, IA: William C. Brown.

Patient Protection and Affordable Care Act, P.L. 111-148, 124 Stat. 119 (March 23, 2010).

Pew Research Center. (2014). *Cell phone and smartphone ownership demographics.* Retrieved from http://www.pewinternet.org/data-trend/mobile/cell-phone-and-smartphone-ownership-demographics/

Seko, Y., Kidd, S., Wiljer, D., & McKenzie, K. (2014). Youth mental health interventions via mobile phones: A scoping review. *Cyberpsychology, Behavior, and Social Networking, 17*, 591–602.

Shore, J. H., Aldag, M., McVeigh, F. L., Hoover, R. L., Ciulla, R., & Fisher, A. (2014). Review of mobile health technology for military mental health. *Military Medicine, 179*, 865–878.

Sieverdes, J. C., Gregoski, M., Patel, S., Williamson, D., Brunner-Jackson, B., Rundbaken, J., et al. (2013). mHealth medication and blood pressure self-management program in Hispanic hypertensives: A proof of concept trial. *Smart Homecare Technology and TeleHealth, 1*, 1–10.

U.S. Census Bureau. (2006). *Hispanic Heritage Month 2005: September 15–October 15* [Press release]. Washington, DC: Public Information Office.

U.S. Department of Health and Human Services. (2012). *Fact sheets: The Affordable Care Act and Latinos.* Retrieved from http://www.hhs.gov/healthcare/

facts/factsheets/2012/04/aca-and-latinos04102012a.html

World Health Organization. (2011). *mHealth: New horizons for health through mobile technologies* (Vol. 3). Geneva: Author.

***

Joyce Y. Lee, MSW, LSW, *is a doctoral student of social work and psychology, School of Social Work, University of Michigan, 1080 South University Avenue, Ann Arbor, MI 48109; e-mail: joyceyl@umich.edu.* ***Sri Harathi, BA,*** *is a research assistant, Department of Psychology, Temple University, Philadelphia.*

Original manuscript received November 4, 2014
Final revision received November 26, 2014
Accepted December 8, 2014
Advance Access Publication November 27, 2015

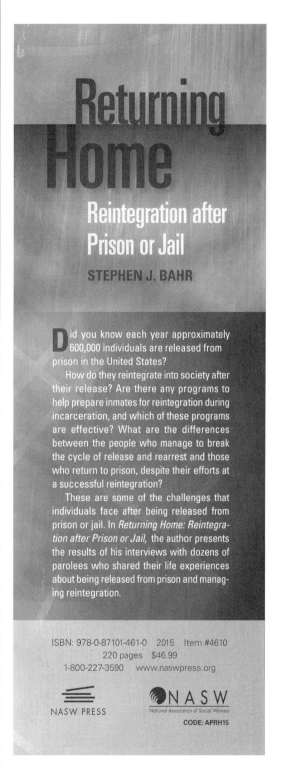

BOOK REVIEW

Losing Tim: How Our Health and Education Systems Failed My Son with Schizophrenia. Paul Gionfriddo. New York: Columbia University Press, 2014, 264 pages. ISBN: 978-0-231-16828-1. $24.95 hardcover.

Losing Tim tells a deeply personal and touching story. The title and organization of the narrative speak to the unfolding, and at times unraveling, of lives shaped both by mental illness and a fragmented system of care. Paul Gionfriddo has the dual perspective of father and legislator who describes his firsthand experiences of how social policies' unintended consequences touched his own life and the life of his son. Gionfriddo speaks frankly of the helplessness and frustration felt as a parent seeking coordinated resources for his child. His clarity of voice and vantage point as a legislator add to the poignancy of this story. Gionfriddo's portrayal of his own experiences crafting and navigating the system as he sought help for his son leaves the reader feeling something has been left unfinished, unconnected, and undone.

Gionfriddo reminds readers that deinstitutionalization has many failings, including that the funding formerly spent on large-scale psychiatric institutions "is spent on hiding people with mental illness behind the bolted doors of our county jails and state prisons" (p. 239). As a social movement, deinstitutionalization has been celebrated as a commitment to helping those with mental illness live successfully in their home communities, with institutional settings closing. When successful, deinstitutionalization leads to an empowered citizenry and richer communities. Gionfriddo's work addresses the stark realities of the practices of deinstitutionalization beyond its philosophical underpinnings and into the real lives of ordinary people affected by underfunded and disconnected systems left behind to take on the functions of dismantled institutions. Gionfriddo makes it clear, stating that

> [when] my home state of Connecticut eliminated most of its state psychiatric hospital beds in the latter part of the twentieth century, we did not replace them with a well-conceived or adequately funded system of community educational, social or behavioral health services and supports. (p. 7)

He adds, "I know this as I was part of this effort as a member of the Connecticut state legislature for eleven years." Recent rulings, such as those related to implementation of the federal *Olmstead v. L.C.* case, indicate ongoing efforts toward deinstitutionalization, similar to those Gionfriddo saw as a legislator (ADA.gov, n.d.).

Early in *Losing Tim*, Gionfriddo makes it clear that he assigns accountability to legislators who defunded the mental health system, citing declining tax bases as well as the lack of political power among mental health consumers and advocacy groups. *Losing Tim* is superior in its account of the flaws of deinstitutionalization and Gionfriddo's recognition of two major oversights in the process. The first, according to Gionfriddo, is an unyielding belief that community-based care is always the best approach, no matter what the conditions of the services, or of the people receiving them. The second, and the heart of the wisdom *Losing Tim* has to offer, is the legislative failure to attend to the fact that those *being* deinstitutionalized during initial policy planning were from a fundamentally different demographic than those who are potentially diverted from psychiatric institutionalization. Tim, after all, was a *child* with mental illness, and his needs were very different from those targeted by most deinstitutionalization efforts. Young adults face similar challenges, seen in the narrative of Tim's story as it unfolds through his transition to adulthood. These young people may have once been institutionalized and possess a complex range of vocational, social, and housing needs that are fundamentally different from those of adults.

The bulk of *Losing Tim* focuses on detailing Gionfriddo's efforts to protect Tim's rights and obtain adequate support for him in the public education system while simultaneously attempting to manage the symptoms of serious mental illness. The tale chronicles numerous difficulties connecting community-based resources with the education system. Among these barriers are lack of adequate time for reviews of Tim's individualized education plan (IEP), lack of institutional knowledge and honoring of the

IEP, deviation from the IEP by teachers and school professionals who viewed Tim's behavior as simply willful, inadequate discipline structures for students with special needs, lack of trauma-informed perspectives or sensitivity to student needs, and the bureaucratic machinery that makes any change slow and arduous. The most salient examples were school personnel's repeated unwillingness to include Tim's community-based therapist in IEP meetings, allowing only 15 minutes for complex IEP meetings, lack of technology support for Tim's learning needs, inability to manage Tim's behavioral needs effectively, placing Tim in close proximity of a peer he feared, and the several months and special hearing requests it took to make even the smallest changes. A chapter aptly titled "Suspended Animation" highlights what amounted to a lost year of education for Tim as Gionfriddo and his wife pursued a due process hearing for help with Tim's IEP. Gionfriddo estimates this cost to be above $100,000. During this hearing a special education teacher testified that Tim's primary diagnosis was "overprotective parents." The comment indicated a lack of both sensitivity and expertise in helping a student with Tim's needs. Furthermore, it appeared that Tim's behaviors were being portrayed as choices, while his parents were being portrayed as unreasonable. As a result of both his struggles and the lack of adequate supports, Tim repeated grades, "never finished a full year of school after the fifth grade" (p. 168), switched high school placements, and tried alternative education. He eventually dropped out with math skills at the fifth-grade level and spelling skills at the third-grade level.

In the latter portion of the book, Gionfriddo details Tim's path to adulthood, which included a series of revolving door experiences of incarceration, homelessness, and transitions in and out of disconnected services. Themes in this section include family disconnection because of confidentiality practices and lack of housing permanency, balancing autonomy and protection for the person with serious mental illness, rigid housing policies and programming rules that may disenfranchise those with the most mental health needs, and low-level crime that leads many with mental illness to frequent interfaces with law enforcement and eventual incarceration. A touching illustration of the folly of housing practices occurred when Tim was evicted with two weeks' notice, and neither he nor his father were notified when his belongings were simply placed on the sidewalk. This was just one of the many losses Tim experienced; no foundation of wellness could be found for Tim to build on.

Ultimately, Gionfriddo's work is largely a foray into the lived experiences of a family grappling with mental illness amid an inadequate support system offering little assistance. They are not alone, given that the Substance Abuse and Mental Health Services Administration (SAMHSA) estimates suggest that 25 percent of people who are homeless struggle with mental illness (SAMHSA, 2011). Many more struggle with incarceration. Countless others are not in a position to tell their stories so eloquently or with such perspective as Gionfriddo.

The book sheds light on gaps in care to which social work students should be exposed. This may be particularly important to emerging social work professionals who may not have knowledge of the systemic history of mental health practices before, during, and after institutionalization, thus limiting their ability to conceptualize these systems of care. It is essential that today's students appreciate that recovery is real, but that institutionalization remains a significant problem for people with serious mental illness. Social work students seeking mental health work must be armed with the tools of advocacy and policy practice to do the necessary work to promote recovery by creating better and integrated community-based supports.

Gionfriddo argues that each person with mental health needs is unique, and because of this, the system cannot be "one size fits all." We must grapple with the reality that there are those who may respond well to prevention, those who need a moderate level of intervention, and those who require long-term care solutions. What these long-term care supports should include and their design is, of course, hotly debated. On this point Gionfriddo excels in pointing out that there are no easy answers. It is not as simple as making clients take their medicine—they may not work, may not be covered by insurance (if the person has it), may cause terrible side effects, or may not be prescribed correctly. In addition, services must include psychosocial supports for housing, socialization, education, vocation, and community integration.

Perhaps the greatest message in Gionfriddo's discussion is the articulation of how fragmented services are for families. In this way, social work students and professionals alike are reminded of the historic role and ethical obligation for advocacy, case management, and other forms of community-based work. Gionfriddo is sharp in his demand for more integrated services and implores social workers and other professionals to recognize that holistic intervention requires support for clients and families in all psychosocial domains and between services providers. The author suggests stepping outside of the tradition of professional siloes to forge meaningful partnerships in mental health, education, and criminal justice to support clients across these systems.

The book is most relevant to social work and social welfare policy practitioners and administrators, particularly those in behavioral health managed-care organizations and public mental health care administration. It is through learning about personal experiences that readers can truly appreciate how policies shape daily living in the most profound ways. Gionfriddo does not devote much space to discussing specific ways to integrate systems of care, nor does he discuss the specific barriers to integration. Thus, this book provides a foundation for an important discussion that readers may feel more compelled to initiate, given how clearly the author details what is broken in our current mental health system. Although the solutions may not be easily forthcoming, Tim's journey illustrates the human suffering, lost potential, and folly of the current system of care for people with serious mental illness that can no longer be accepted as simply a better alternative to institutionalization. Should the irrationality and inhumane nature of the current arrangement fail to move Gionfriddo's readers, they need only consider the immense costs of educating, housing, incarcerating, and treating Tim and the many others like him in these various systems. HSW

REFERENCES

ADA.gov. (n.d.). *Information and technical assistance on the Americans with Disabilities Act. Olmstead: Community integration for everyone.* Retrieved from http://www.ada.gov/olmstead/

Substance Abuse and Mental Health Services Administration. (2011, July). *Current statistics on the prevalence and characteristics of people experiencing homelessness in the United States.* Retrieved from http://homeless.samhsa.gov/ResourceFiles/hrc_factsheet.pdf

Mandy Ann Fauble, PhD
Edinboro University
Edinboro, PA

Advance Access Publication November 27, 2015

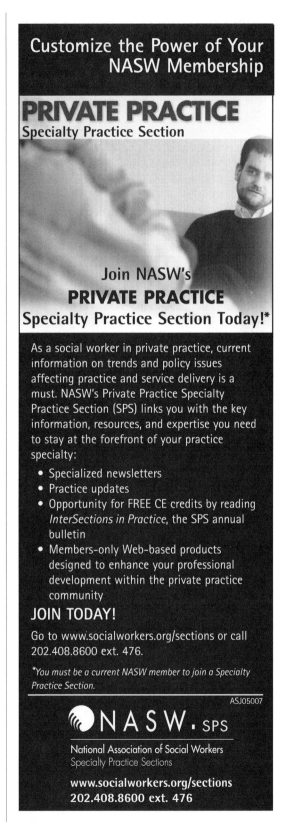

BURNOUT AND SELF-CARE in Social Work

A GUIDEBOOK FOR STUDENTS AND THOSE IN MENTAL HEALTH AND RELATED PROFESSIONS

SARAKAY SMULLENS

Are you exhausted, stressed, overwhelmed? Or do you feel that these reactions are very close, waiting in the wings? If so, *Burnout and Self-Care in Social Work* is the book for you. Burnout, one of the primary reasons why committed social workers leave the profession, is a grave and pervasive problem with glaring impact. Those entering social work and all related fields, as well as those already deeply involved, must be educated about its toll and prepared to address and prevent the depletion it causes. This book provides valuable insights for all who carry complex and divergent responsibilities. SaraKay Smullens addresses both burnout and self-care from a professional, personal, social, and physical perspective. She integrates research, case studies, questionnaire responses, and her seasoned experience to identify three major root causes of burnout—compassion fatigue, countertransference, and vicarious trauma—and defines creative strategies for individual self-care opportunities. This resourceful guide offers clarification, direction, and opportunity for reflection to help students and professionals in social work, related fields, and beyond find balance in their personal and professional lives as well as ease work-related stress to better serve clients—and, in this way, achieve professional equilibrium, success, and personal fulfillment.

> *Burnout and Self-Care in Social Work is an engrossing and comprehensive treatment of a most critical and complex topic in social work today. Service providers will undoubtedly benefit from SaraKay Smullens's insights into recognizing and overcoming burnout and equipping oneself with the tools to build self-care into the heart of one's practice. This fundamental self-actualization is the cornerstone of any truly successful individual within the social work profession and beyond.*
>
> JOHN L. JACKSON, JR., PHD
> DEAN, SCHOOL OF SOCIAL POLICY & PRACTICE
> RICHARD PERRY UNIVERSITY PROFESSOR
> UNIVERSITY OF PENNSYLVANIA

NASW PRESS

ISBN: 978-0-87101-462-7. 2015. Item #4627. 152 pages. $34.99.
1-800-227-3590 • www.naswpress.org

NASW
National Association of Social Workers

CODE APBO15

HEALTH & SOCIAL WORK

Health & Social Work, established in 1976, is a professional journal committed to improving social work practice and expanding knowledge in health care. It is written for workers in all areas of the physiological, psychological, social, cultural, and environmental health sciences. Health is defined broadly to include both physical and mental health. The editorial board welcomes manuscripts on all aspects of health that are of professional concern to social workers. The journal carries articles on practice, social policy and planning, legislative issues, innovations in health care, and research.

The editorial board of *Health & Social Work* strives to include articles that appeal to its broad constituency, addressing both practice and policy issues. Related articles are often grouped in an issue. A call for papers on special themes may be issued on topics of major importance to the field, such as substance abuse or mental health.

Reviewers look for submissions to

- be important to social work and relevant to health
- contain a clear statement of purpose and a consistent focus
- expand current knowledge
- build on the work of others
- contain a current and appropriate literature review
- include relevant medical information, such as etiology, prognosis, and hereditary factors, if disease specific
- present complete methodology for a research article
- be well organized, with a logical, orderly presentation
- support conclusions with data or a logical argument
- contain a clear explication of the implications for social work.

ARTICLES

Manuscripts for full-length articles **may not exceed 20 pages,** including all components. The entire review process is anonymous. At least three reviewers critique each manuscript, after which the editor-in-chief makes a decision, taking those reviews into consideration.

COLUMNS

Practice Forum offers authors the opportunity to describe practice innovations and action research. It is designed to publish material that is important to and written by practitioners. Submissions should describe new and effective programs, techniques, or policies. The editor of the Practice Forum may assist authors in developing articles for the column. **Practice Forum submissions may be no longer than eight pages.**

National Health Line reports current legislative and political issues that have implications for social work practice in health settings. It provides a link between social work practice and health care policy. Written by the column editor, National Health Line presents contemporary issues that could have the greatest impact on social work clients. Suggestions for topics to be covered are invited.

Viewpoint features readers' comments and opinions on current issues in the profession. It offers writers an opportunity to express their opinion on issues that may have an impact on social work or social work clients in health or mental health settings. **Viewpoint submissions may be no longer than seven pages.**

Letters to the Editor enhance professional dialogue by providing readers the opportunity to comment on issues covered in the journal or other points of interest to social workers in health or mental health settings. Although we acknowledge and read all letters, not all can be published. Letters selected by the editor-in-chief may be shortened to fit the available space. **Letters to the Editor submissions may be no longer than two pages.**

To prepare your manuscript in the proper format for submission view *Writing for NASW Press: Information for Authors,* at our Web site at www.naswpress.org. Please submit manuscripts as Word documents through the online submission portal at http://hsw.msubmit.net (initial, one-time registration is required).